CW00829762

ISBN: 9781313878456

Published by:
HardPress Publishing
8345 NW 66TH ST #2561
MIAMI FL 33166-2626

Email: info@hardpress.net
Web: http://www.hardpress.net

THE LONE STAR DEFENDERS

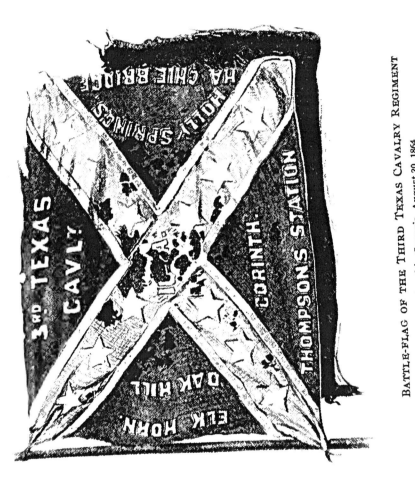

BATTLE-FLAG OF THE THIRD TEXAS CAVALRY REGIMENT

Captured in Georgia. August 20, 1864

THE LONE STAR DEFENDERS

A CHRONICLE OF THE THIRD TEXAS CAVALRY, ROSS' BRIGADE

BY

S. B. BARRON

OF THE
THIRD TEXAS CAVALRY

NEW YORK AND WASHINGTON
THE NEALE PUBLISHING COMPANY
1908

CONTENTS

3

CHAPTER IV

THE WAR IN MISSOURI

CHAPTER V

THE WAR IN MISSOURI—*Continued*

CHAPTER VI

THE SIEGE OF CORINTH

CHAPTER VII

BATTLE OF IUKA

CONTENTS 5

CHAPTER XII

BATTLE AT YAZOO CITY

CHAPTER XIII

UNDER FIRE FOR ONE HUNDRED DAYS

CHAPTER XIV

KILPATRICK'S RAID

CHAPTER XV

UNION SOLDIER'S ACCOUNT OF KILPATRICK'S RAID

CHAPTER XVI

CLOSE OF THE ATLANTA CAMPAIGN

PAGE

Sherman Changes His Tactics—Hood Deceived—Heavy Fighting—Atlanta Surrenders—End of the Campaign—Losses—Scouting—An Invader's Devastation—Raiding the Raiders—Hood Crosses the Coosa—A Reconnoissance—Negro Spies—Raiding the Blacks—Crossing Indian Creek—A Conversion . . . .

CHAPTER XVII

MY LAST BATTLE

Tories and Deserters—A Tragic Story—A Brutal Murder—The Son's Vow—Vengeance—A Southern Heroine—Seeking Our Command—Huntsville—A Strange Meeting—We Find the Division—The Battle in the Fog—My Last Battle . . . .

CHAPTER XVIII

ROSS' REPORT OF BRIGADE'S LAST CAMPAIGN

Ross' Report—Repulse a Reconnoitering Party—Effective Fighting Strength—Advance Guard—The Battle at Campbellsville—Results—Thompson's Station—Harpeth River—Murfreesboro—Lynville—Pulaski—Sugar Creek—Losses During Campaign—Captures—Acknowledgments . . . .

CHAPTER XIX

THE END OF THE WAR

Christmas—I Lose All My Belongings—The "Owl Train"—A Wedding—Furloughed—Start for Texas—Hospitality—A Night in the Swamp—The Flooded Country—Swimming the Rivers—In Texas—Home Again—Surrender of Lee, Johnston, and Kirby Smith—Copy of Leave of Absence—Recapitulation—Valuation of Horses in 1864—Finis . . . . .

ILLUSTRATIONS

INTRODUCTION

As my recollections of the war between the States, or the Confederate War, in which four of the best years of my life (May, 1861, to May, 1865) were given to the service of the Confederate States of America, are to be written at the earnest request of my children, and mainly for their gratification, it is, perhaps, proper to preface the recital by going back a few years in order to give a little family history.

I was born in what is now the suburbs of the town of Gurley in Madison County, Alabama, on the 9th day of November, 1834. My father, Samuel Boulds Barron, was born in South Carolina in 1793. His father, James Barron, as I understand, was a native of Ireland. My mother's maiden name was Martha Cotten, daughter of James Cotten, who was from Guilford County, North Carolina, and who was in the battle of Guilford Court House, at the age of sixteen. His future wife, Nancy Johnson, was then a young girl living in hearing of the battle at the Court House. About the beginning of the past century, 1800, my Grandfather Cotten, with his wife, her brother Abner Johnson, and their relatives, Gideon and William Pillow, and their sister, Mrs. Dew, moved out from North Carolina into Tennessee, stopping in Davidson County, near Nashville. Later Abner Johnson and the Pillows settled in Maury County, near Columbia, and about the year 1808 my grandfather and his family came on to Madison County, Alabama, and settled at what has always been known as Cave Springs, about fifteen miles east or southeast from Huntsville. In the second war with Great Britain (the War of 1812) my Grandfather Cotten again answered the call to arms, and as a captain he served his country with notable gallantry.

It is like an almost forgotten dream, the recollection of my paternal grandmother and my maternal grandfather, for both of them died when I was a small child. My maternal grandmother, however, who lived to the age of eighty-seven years, I remember well. In my earliest recollection my father was a school-teacher, teaching at a village then called "The Section," afterwards "Lowsville," being now the town of Maysville, twelve miles east of Huntsville. He was well-educated and enjoyed the reputation of being an excellent teacher. He quit teaching, however, and settled on a small farm four miles east of Cave Springs, on what is known as the "Cove road," running from Huntsville to Bellefonte. Here he died when I was about seven years of age, leaving my mother with five children: John Ashworth, a son by her first husband; my brother, William J. Barron, who now lives in Huntsville, Alabama; two sisters, Tabitha and Nancy Jane; and myself. About nine years later our mother died. In the meantime our half-brother had arrived at man's estate and left home. Soon after our mother's death we sold the homestead, and each one went his or her way, as it were, the sisters living with our near-by relatives until they married. My brother and myself found employment in Huntsville and lived there. Our older sister and her husband came to Texas in about the year 1857, and settled first in Nacogdoches County. In the fall of 1859 I came to Texas, to bring my then widowed sister and her child to my sister already here. And so, as the old song went, " I am away here in Texas."

The Lone Star Defenders

CHAPTER I

THE OUTBREAK OF THE WAR

Journey to Texas—John Brown's Raid—My Secession Resolution—Presidential Election—Lincoln Elected—Excitement in the South—Secession Ordinances—" The Lone Star Defenders "—Fort Sumter Fired On—Camp Life—The Regiment Complete—Citizens' Kindness—Mustered In—The Third Texas Cavalry—Roster.

No, I am not going to write, or attempt to write, a history of the war, or even a detailed account of any campaign or battle in which I participated, but only mean to set forth the things which I witnessed or experienced myself in the four years of marching, camping, and fighting, as I can now recall them —only, or mainly, personal reminiscences. Incidentally I will give the names of my comrades of Company C, Third Texas Cavalry, and tell, so far as I can remember, what became of the individuals who composed the company. I will not dwell on the causes of the war or anything which has been so often and so well told relating thereto, but will merely state that I had always been very conservative in my feelings in political matters, and was so all through the exciting times just preceding the war while Abolitionism and Secession were so much discussed by our statesmen, orators, newspapers, and periodicals. I had witnessed the Kansas troubles, which might be called a skirmish before the battle, with much interest and anxiety, and without losing faith in the ability and wisdom of our statesmen to settle the existing troubles without disrupting the government. But on my journey to Texas, as we glided down the Mississippi from Memphis to New Orleans, on board the *Lizzie Simmons*, a new and beautiful steamer, afterwards converted into a cotton-clad Confederate gunboat, we obtained New Orleans papers from an up-river boat. The papers contained an account of John Brown's raid on Harper's Ferry. I read this, and became a Secessionist. I saw, or thought I saw, that the storm was coming, that it was inevitable, and it seemed useless to shut my eyes longer to the fact.

The year 1860, my first in Texas, was a memorable one in several respects, not only to the newcomers but to the oldest inhabitant. The severest drouth ever known in eastern Texas prevailed until after the middle of August. It was the hottest summer ever known in Texas, the temperature in July running up to 112 degrees in the shade. It was a Presidential election year, and political excitement was intense. The Democrats were divided, while the Abolitionists had nominated Abraham Lincoln as their candidate for President, with a good prospect of electing him by a sectional vote. Several towns in Texas being almost destroyed by fire during the extreme heat of the summer, an impression became generally prevalent that Northern incendiaries were prowling through the State burning property and endeavoring to incite the negroes to insurrection. The excitement, apprehension, unrest, and the vague fear of unseen danger pervading the minds of the people of Texas cannot be understood by persons who were not in the State at that time. The citizens organized patrol forces and armed men guarded the towns, day and night, for weeks. Every passing stranger was investigated and his credentials examined. The poor peddler, especially, was in imminent danger of being mobbed at any time on mere suspicion.

At the November election Abraham Lincoln was elected President. This was considered by the Secessionists as an overt act on the part of the North that would justify secession. I was out in the country when the news of the election came, and when, on my return, I rode into Rusk the Lone Star flag was floating over the court-house and Abraham Lincoln, in effigy, was hanging to the limb of a sweet gum tree that stood near the northwest corner of the court yard. From this time excitement ran high. Immediate steps were taken by the extreme Southern States to secede from the Union, an act that was consummated as soon as practicable by the assembling of State conventions and the passage of ordinances of secession. Now, too, volunteer companies began organizing in order to be ready for the conflict which seemed to be inevitable.

We soon raised a company in Rusk for the purpose of drilling and placing ourselves in readiness for the first call for troops from Texas. We organized by electing General Joseph L. Hogg, father of Ex-Governor J. S. Hogg, as captain. The company was named " The Lone Star Defenders," for every company must needs have a name in those days. Early in 1861, however, when it appeared necessary to prepare for actual service, the company was reorganized and the gallant Frank M. Taylor made captain, as General Hogg was not expected to enter the army as captain. Several of the States had already seceded, the military posts in the South were being captured by the Confederates and Fort Sumter, in Charleston Harbor, was fired upon by our General Beauregard on the 12th day of April, 1861. The dogs of war were turned loose. War now became a stern reality, a war the magnitude of which no one then had any conception. President Lincoln's first call for volunteers was for ninety-day men, and the Confederate volunteers were mustered in for one year.

Having learned that Elkanah Greer, of Marshall, had been commissioned colonel and ordered to raise a regiment of Texas cavalry, we lost no time in reporting ourselves ready to make one company of the regiment, and soon received instructions to report at Dallas, on a certain day in June, when a regiment would be formed. So on Monday morning, June 10, in the year of our Lord, 1861, we were to leave, and did leave, Rusk for Dallas—and beyond, as the exigencies of the war might determine. The population of the town, men, women, and children, were on the streets, in tears, to bid us farewell. Even rough, hard-faced men whose appearance would lead one to believe they hadn't shed a tear since their boyhood, boo-hoo'd and were unable to speak the word " good-by." This day of leave-taking was the saddest of the war to many of us.

After we had mounted our horses we assembled around the front of the old Thompson Hotel, which stood where the Acme Hotel now stands, when our old friend, General Hogg, standing on the front steps, delivered us a formal and a very tender farewell address. War was not unknown to him, for he had been a soldier in the early days of Texas, as well as a member of the Texas Congress in the days of the republic. He was a fine specimen of the best type of Southern manhood—tall, slender, straight as an Indian, and exceedingly dignified in his manner. As brave as " Old Hickory," he often reminded me of the pictures I had seen of General Jackson, and he certainly had many similar traits of character. We venerated, admired, and loved him, and he was warmly attached to the company. In his address he gave us much good advice, even to the details of mess duties and the treatment of our messmates. Among other things, he said, " Don't ever jeer at or mock any of your comrades who cannot stand the fire of the enemy. Some of you, perhaps, will find yourselves unable to do so. Some men are thus constituted without knowing it, until they are tried. So you should be charitable towards such unfortunates." Later I found these words of our old soldier friend to be true. This ceremony ended, we sadly moved off by twos, over the hill, and up the street leading into the Jacksonville road.

As we marched forward sadness was soon succeeded by merriment and good cheer. Some of the boys composed a little song, which was frequently sung by I. K. Frazer and others as we went marching on. It began:

" The Lone Star Defenders, a gallant little band,
  On the tenth of June left their native land."

Before leaving home we had spent two weeks in a camp of instruction, and learned something of the duties of camp life and the necessary art of rolling and unrolling our blankets. We camped the first night near Jorial Barnett's, between Jacksonville and Larissa. Two of the Barnett boys were going with us, and several from Larissa. When we reached Larissa next morning we there found a young man, Charley Watts, who was a bugler, and had been in the Federal Army, he said. He was willing and anxious to go with us, and we wanted him, as he was young and active, but he was afoot, and seemed to own nothing beyond his wearing apparel. So we appealed to the citizens, as a goodly number had gathered into the little village to see the soldiers pass, and in little more time than it takes to tell it, we had him rigged with horse, bridle, saddle, and blankets. Charley proved to be a fine bugler, the finest bugler I ever heard in either army, and he was a most gallant young fellow. We moved on, bidding farewell to Captain Taylor's noble and patriotic old mother, as we passed her residence.

Fearing we might be left out of the regiment, we dispatched Captain Taylor and one or two others well-mounted men to go ahead and secure and hold our place for us. The ladies of Cherokee County having presented us with a beautiful flag, this we unfurled and marched through the towns and villages along the way in great style and military pomp. At Kaufman we received quite an ovation. Arriving there about ten o'clock in the morning, we were met by a deputation of citizens, who invited us to dine at the hotel at the expense of the town.

This was very reluctantly declined, for we were afraid of losing time. Poor fellows, we often regretted missing that good dinner, and we really had plenty of time, if we had only known it. To show our appreciation of their hospitality we marched around the public square, displaying the flag and sounding the bugle. When we had arrived in front of a saloon we were halted and all invited to dismount and drink, without cost to us. We here spent perhaps an hour, during which time numbers of the boys entered stores to purchase small necessary articles, and in every instance pay was declined.

In due time we went into camp in a post oak grove two miles east of Dallas, a locality, by the way, which is now well within the city limits. And here we remained for some time.

Eight other organized companies were soon camped in different localities in the neighborhood, but we were still one company short. However, as there were many men, including a large squad from Kaufman County, some from Cherokee and other counties, on the ground wishing to go with us, and who could not get into the organized companies because they were all full, they organized themselves into a tenth company, which completed the necessary number for the regiment.

We spent about four weeks in Dallas County, a delay caused in good part by the necessity of waiting for the arrival of a train from San Antonio carrying United States wagons and mules captured at that post by the Confederates. The time, however, was well spent in daily drills, in feeding, grazing and attending to our horses; and then, too, we were learning valuable lessons in camp life. While here we had plenty of rations for ourselves and plenty of forage for the horses.

The citizens of Dallas County, as far as we came in contact with them, were very kind to us. Our nearest neighbor was a German butcher by the name of Nusbauman. We used water from the well in his yard and were indebted to him and his family for many acts of kindness.

On one occasion Mrs. Nusbauman complained to Captain Taylor that one of his men had borrowed her shears to cut hair with, and would not bring them back. No, she did not know the name of the offender. The captain then said, " Madame, do you know the man when you see him? " " Oh, yes." " Well, when he comes to draw water again you sprinkle flour on his back and I will find your shears." In a few hours one of the men came out from the well with his back covered with flour—and the shears were promptly returned.

Our next nearest neighbors were a family named Sheppard, who lived a few hundred yards south of our camp, and whose kindness was unbounded. Their house was our hospital for the time we were in their vicinity, and the three young ladies of the family, Misses Jennie Wood, Maggie, and another, were unremitting in their attentions to the sick. On one damp, drizzly day when I had a chill they heard of it, somehow, and in the afternoon two of them drove up in a buggy and called for me to go home with them, where I could be sheltered, as we yet had no tents. I went, of course, recovered in one day,

convalesced in about three days, and reluctantly returned to camp.   In an effort to do some washing
for myself, I had lost a plain gold ring from my
finger, a present from Miss Cattie Everett of Rusk,
and Miss Jennie Wood Sheppard replaced it with
one of her own.   This ring was worn by me continually, not only during the war, but for several
years after its close.

I do not remember the date, but some day near the
end of June " The Lone Star Defenders," that " gallant little band," were formally mustered into the
service of the Confederate States of America, for
one year.   We were subjected to no physical examination, or other foolishness, but every fellow was
taken for better or for worse, and no questions were
asked, except the formal, " Do you solemnly swear,"
etc.   The company was lettered " C," Greer's Regiment, Texas Cavalry—afterwards numbered and
ever afterwards known as the Third Texas Cavalry.
We were mustered in, officers and men, as follows:

Officers—Frank M. Taylor, captain; James J. A.
Barker, first lieutenant; Frank M. Daniel, second
lieutenant; James A. Jones, second lieutenant; Wallace M. Caldwell, orderly sergeant; John D. White,
second sergeant; S. B. Barron, third sergeant; Tom
Petree, fourth sergeant; William Pennington, first
corporal; Thomas F. Woodall, second corporal; C.
C. Acker, third corporal; P. C. Coupland, fourth
corporal; Charles Watts, bugler; John A. Boyd,
ensign.

Privates—Peter Acker, John B. Armstrong,
David H. Allen, James M. Brittain, R. L. Barnett,
James Barnett, Severe D. Box, A. A. Box, William

P. Bowers, John W. Baker, C. C. Brigman, George F. Buxton, Jordan Bass, Carter Caldwell, William P. Crawley, A. G. Carmichael, A. M. Croft, James P. Chester, Leander W. Cole, James W. Cooper, William H. Carr, W. J. Davis, James E. Dillard, F. M. Dodson, John E. Dunn, O. M. Doty, H. H. Donoho, B. C. Donald, Stock Ewin, John J. Felps, I. K. Frazer, John Germany, Luther Grimes, E. M. Grimes, J. H. Gum, L. F. Grisham, W. L. Gammage, W. D. Herndon, J. R. Halbert, W. T. Harris, D. B. Harris, Thomas E. Hogg, John Honson, Warren H. Higginbotham, R. H. Hendon, William Hammett, James B. Hardgrave, Felix G. Hardgrave, R. L. Hood, William Hood, James Ivy, Thomas J. Johnson, J. H. Jones, John B. Long, Ben A. Long, George C. Long, R. C. Lawrence, John Lambert, J. B. Murphy, William P. Mosely, John Meyers, Harvey N. Milligan, W. C. McCain, G. A. McKee, W. W. McDugald, Dan McCaskill, Samuel W. Newberry, William A. Newton, George Noland, Baxter Newman, J. T. Park, T. A. Putnam, Lemon R. Peacock, W. T. Phillips, Lemuel H. Reed, T. W. Roberts, Cythe Robertson, Calvin M. Roark, John B. Reagan, A. B. Summers, John W. Smith, Cicero H. Smith, Rufus Smith, Sam E. Scott, J. R. Starr, James R. Taylor, Reuben G. Thompson, Dan H. Turney, Robert F. Woodall, Woodson O. Wade, F. M. Wade, E. S. Wallace, R. S. Wallace, John R. Watkins, C. C. Watkins, Joe L. Welch, Thomas H. Willson, N. J. Yates.

Total rank and file—112 men.

In addition to the above list of original members, the following named recruits were added to the com-

PETER F. ROSS
Major and Lieutenant-Colonel Sixth Texas Cavalry

FACING 24

pany after we had lost several of our men by death and discharge:

A. J. Gray, Charles B. Harris, J. T. Halbert, John E. Jones, Wm. H. Kellum, W. S. Keahey, S. N. Keahey, J. D. Miller, T. L. Newman, T. L. Nosworthy, John W. Wade, Wyatt S. Williams, Eugene W. Williams.

Total—125 men enlisted in the company.

Of these the killed numbered	14
Died of disease	16
Discharged	31
Commissioned officers resigned	3
Missing and never heard of	2
Deserted	7
Survived (commissioned and non-commissioned officers, 12; privates, 40)	52
	125

Of these recruits, six, the first on the list, came to us in February and March, 1862; the next three joined us in April, 1862; the remaining four joined us in 1863, while we were in Mississippi.

The company consisted mainly of natives of the different Southern States, with a few native Texans. Aside from these we had Buxton, from the State of Maine; Milligan, from Indiana, and three foreigners, William Hood, an Englishman; John Dunn, Irish, and John Honson, a Swede. Milligan was a printer, and being too poor to buy his outfit when he joined us, he was furnished with horse and accouterments by our friend, B. Miller, a German citizen of Rusk.

CHAPTER II

OFF FOR THE FRONT

Organization of Regiment—Officers—Accouterment—On the March—Taming a Trouble-maker—Crossing the Red River —In the Indian Territory—The Indian Maid—Fort Smith—The March to Missouri—McCulloch's Headquarters—Under Orders—Preparation for First Battle.

AFTER the companies were mustered into the service the regiment was organized. Colonel Elkanah Greer was commissioned by the Confederate War Department. Walter P. Lane was elected lieutenant-colonel, and George W. Chilton, father of United States Senator Horace Chilton, was made major. M. D. Ecton, first lieutenant of Company B, was made adjutant, Captain ———— Harris, quartermaster, Jas. B. Armstrong, of Henderson, commissary, and our Dr. W. W. McDugald, surgeon.

Thus was organized the first regiment to leave the State of Texas, and one of the best regiments ever in the Confederate service. I would not say that it was the *best* regiment, as in my opinion the best regiment and the bravest man in the Confederate Army were hard to find. That is to say, no one regiment was entitled to be designated " the best regiment," as no one of our brave men could rightly be designated " the bravest man in the army." Napoleon called Marshal Ney " the bravest of the brave," but no one could single out a

Confederate soldier and truthfully say, " He is the bravest man in the army." It was unfortunately true that all our men were not brave and trustworthy, for we had men who were too cowardly to fight, and we had some men unprincipled enough to desert; but taken all in all, for gallantry and for fighting qualities under any and all circumstances, either in advance or retreat, the regiment deservedly stood in the front rank in all our campaigning.

The regiment was well officered, field staff, and line. Colonel Greer was a gallant man, but unfortunately his mind was too much bent on a brigadier's stars; Major Chilton, whenever an opportunity offered, showed himself to be brave and gallant; but Walter P. Lane, our lieutenant-colonel, was the life of the regiment during our first year's service. A more gallant man than he never wore a sword, bestrode a war horse, or led a regiment in battle. He was one of the heroes of San Jacinto, and a born soldier. In camps, in times when there was little or nothing to do, he was not overly popular with the men, but when the fighting time came he gained the admiration of everyone.

At last the long-looked-for train came—United States wagons drawn by six-mule teams, poor little Spanish or Mexican mules, driven by Mexicans. They brought us tents, camp kettles, mess pans and such things, and for arms, holster pistols. We were furnished with two wagons to the company and were given Sibley tents,—large round tents that would protect sixteen men with their arms and accouterments,—a pair of holster pistols apiece, and a fair outfit of " cooking tricks." We were then formed

into messes of sixteen men each, and each mess was
provided with the Sibley tent, the officers being
provided with wall tents.   Fairly mounted, we were
pretty well equipped now, our chief deficiency being
the very poor condition of the mules and the lack of
proper arms, for the men, in mustering, had gathered
up shotguns, rifles, and any kind of gun obtainable
at home, many of them being without a firearm of
any kind.   A large number had had huge knives
made in the blacksmith shops, with blade eighteen
to twenty-four inches long, shaped something like a
butcher's cleaver, keen-edged, with a stout handle, a
weapon after the order of a Cuban machete.   These
were carried in leather scabbards, hung to the saddle, and with these deadly weapons the boys expected
to ride through the ranks of the Federal armies and
chop down the men right and left.   Now, however,
to this equipment were added the pair of holster pistols.   These very large, brass-mounted, single-bar-
reled pistols—with barrels about a foot long—carried a large musket ball, and were suspended in hol-
sters that fitted over the horn of the saddle, thus
placing them in a convenient position for use.   In
addition to all this, every fellow carried a grass
rope at least forty feet long and an iron stake pin.
These latter were for staking out the horses to
graze, and many was the untrained horse that paid
dear for learning the art of " walking the rope,"
for an educated animal would never injure himself
in the least.

All things being ready, we now started on our
long march, accompanied by Captain J. J. Goode's
battery, which had been organized at Dallas, to join

General Ben McCulloch in northwestern Arkansas, where he, with what forces he had been able to gather, was guarding our Arkansas frontier. Leaving Dallas on the —— day of July, we moved via McKinney and Sherman, crossing Red River at Colbert's ferry, thence by the overland mail route through the Indian Territory to Fort Smith, Ark., and beyond. We made moderate marches, the weather being very warm, and we then had no apparent reason for rapid movements.

When near McKinney we stopped two or three days. Here our man from the State of Maine began to give us trouble. When sober, Buxton was manageable and a useful man to the company, but when he was in liquor, which was any time he could get whisky, he was troublesome, quarrelsome, and dangerous, especially to citizens. One afternoon Captain Taylor and myself rode into McKinney, where we found Buxton drunk and making trouble. The captain ordered him to camp, but he contumaciously refused to go. We managed to get him back to the rear of a livery stable, near a well, and Captain Taylor forced him down across a mound of fertilizer—holding him there. Then he ordered me to pour water on Buxton, which I did most copiously. I drew bucket after bucket of cold water from the well and poured it upon Buxton's prostrate, soldierly form, until he was thoroughly cooled and partially sobered, when the captain let him up and again ordered him to camp—and he went, cursing and swearing vengeance. This man, after giving us a good deal of trouble from time to time until after the battle of Elkhorn in the spring of 1862, was jailed in Fort Smith for shooting a citizen in the street, and here we left him and crossed the Mississippi River. He made his escape from jail and followed us to the State of Mississippi, when Lieutenant-Colonel Lane ordered him out of camp. He afterwards returned to Rusk, where he was killed one day by a gunshot wound, but by whom no one seemed to know.

We passed through Sherman early in the morning, and I stopped to have my horse shod, overtaking the command at Colbert's ferry in the afternoon, when they were crossing Red River. The day was fair, the weather dry and hot. The river, very low now, had high banks, and in riding down from the south side you came on to a wide sandbar extending to a narrow channel running against the north bank, where a small ferryboat was carrying the wagons and artillery across. A few yards above the ferry the river was easily fordable, so the horsemen had all crossed and gone into camp a mile beyond the river, as had most of the wagons. I rode to the other side and stopped on the north bank to watch operations.

All the wagons but one had been ferried over, and this last one had been driven down on the sandbar near the ferry landing, waiting for the boat's return, while two pieces of artillery were standing near by on the sandbar. Suddenly I heard a roaring sound up the river, as if a wind storm was coming. I looked in that direction and saw a veritable flood rushing down like a mighty wave of the sea, roaring and foaming as it came. The driver of the team standing near the water saw it and instinctively began turning his team to drive out, but, realizing that this would be impossible, he detached his mules and with his utmost efforts was only able to save the team, while every available man had to lend assistance in order to save the two pieces of artillery. In five minutes' time, perhaps, the water had risen fifteen to eighteen feet, and the banks were full of muddy, rushing water, and remained so as long as we were there. The wagon, which belonged to the quartermaster, was swept off by the tide and lost, with all its contents. It stood in its position until the water rose to the top of the cover, when it floated off.

After camping for the night, we moved on. As we were now in the Indian Territory, the young men were all on the look-out for the beautiful Indian girls of whom they had read so much, and I think some of them had waived the matter of engagement before leaving home until they could determine whether they would prefer marrying some of the pretty girls that were so numerous in this Indian country. We had not gone far on our march when we met a Chickasaw damsel. She was rather young in appearance, of medium height, black unkempt hair, black eyes, high cheekbones, and was bareheaded and bare-footed. Her dress was of some well-worn cotton fabric, of a color hard to define, rather an earthy color. In style it was of the extreme low neck and short kind, and a semi-bloomer. Of other wearing apparel it is unnecessary to speak, unless you wish a description of another Indian. This one was too sensible to weight herself with a multiplicity of garments in July. She was a regular middle of the roader, as she stuck close to that part of the Territory strictly.   As we were marching by twos we separated and left her to that part of the highway which she seemed to like best.   She continued her walk westwardly as we continued our march eastwardly, turning her head right and left, to see what manner of white soldiers the Confederate Government was sending out.   This gave all an opportunity to glimpse at her charms.   Modestly she walked along without speaking to any of us, as we had never been introduced to her.   Only one time did I hear her speak a word, and that was apparently to herself.   As Lieutenant Daniel passed her with his long saber rattling, she exclaimed, in good English: " *Pretty white man!*—got big knife! "

As we went marching on the conversation became more general; that is, more was said about the beautiful country, the rich lands and fine cattle, and not so much about beautiful Indian girls.   But every fellow kept his eye to the front, expecting we would meet scores of girls, perhaps hundreds, but all were disappointed, as this was the only full-blooded Indian we met in the highway from Colbert's ferry to Fort Smith.   The fact is, the Indians shun white people who travel the main road. Away out in the prairie some two hundred yards you will find Indian trails running parallel with the road, and the Indians keep to these trails to avoid meeting the whites.   If they chance to live in a hut near the road you find no opening toward the road, and, if approached, they will deny that they can speak English, when, in fact, they speak it readily and plainly.

One day I came up with one of our teamsters in trouble. He needed an ax to cut down a sapling, so I galloped back to an Indian's hut near by, and as there was no enclosure, rode around to the door. The Indian came out and I asked him to lend me an ax a few minutes. He shook his head and said, " Me no intender," again and again, and this was the only word I could get out of him until I dismounted and picked up the ax, which was lying on the ground near the door. He then began, in good English, to beg me not to take his ax. I carried it to the teamster, however, but returned it to the Indian in a few minutes.

There are, or were then, people of mixed blood living along the road in good houses and in good style, where travelers could find entertainment. Numbers of these had small Confederate flags flying over the front gateposts—and all seemed to be loyal to our cause. Two young Choctaws joined one of our companies and went with us, one of them remaining with us during the war, and an excellent soldier he was, too.

At Boggy Depot the ladies presented us with a beautiful flag, which was carried until it was many times pierced with bullets, the staff shot in two, and the flag itself torn into shreds. Arriving at Big Blue River, we lost one or two horses in crossing, by drowning. But finally we reached Fort Smith, on a Saturday, remaining there until Monday morning.

While in the Choctaw Nation our men had the opportunity of attending an Indian war dance, and added to their fitness for soldiers by learning the warwhoop, which many of them were soon able to give just as real Indians do.

Fort Smith, a city of no mean proportions, is situated on the south bank of the Arkansas River, very near the line of the Indian Territory.   Another good town, Van Buren, is situated on the north bank of the river, five miles below Fort Smith.   While we were at Fort Smith orders came from General McCulloch, then in southwest Missouri, to cut loose from all incumbrances and hasten to his assistance as rapidly as possible, as a battle was imminent. Consequently, leaving all trains, baggage, artillery, all sick and disabled men and horses to follow us as best they could, we left on Monday morning in the lightest possible marching order, for a forced march into Missouri.   Our road led across Boston Mountain, through Fayetteville and Cassville, on towards Springfield.   Crossing the river at Van Buren, we began the march over the long, hot, dry, and fearfully dusty road.   As we passed through Van Buren I heard " Dixie " for the first time, played by a brass band.   Some of the boys obtained the words of the song, and then the singers gave us " Dixie " morning, noon, and night, and sometimes between meals.   This march taxed my physical endurance to the utmost, and in the evening, when orders came to break ranks and camp, I sometimes felt as if I could not march one mile farther.   The first or orderly sergeant and second sergeant having been left behind with the train, the orderly sergeant's duties fell upon me, which involved looking after forage and rations, and other offices, after the day's march.

On Saturday noon we were at Cassville, Mo.
That night we marched nearly all night, lying down
in a stubble field awhile before daylight, where we
slept two or three hours. About ten o'clock Sunday
morning, tired, dusty, hungry, and sleepy, we went
into camp in the neighborhood of General McCulloch's headquarters, in a grove of timber near a
beautiful, clear, little stream. The first thing we
did was to look after something to eat for ourselves
and horses, as we had had no food since passing
Cassville, and only a very light lunch then. The
next thing was to go in bathing, and wash our
clothes, as we had had no change, and then to get
some longed-for sleep. In the meantime Colonel
Greer had gone up to General McCulloch's headquarters to report our arrival. I was not present
at the interview, but I imagine it ran something like
this, as they knew each other well. Colonel Greer
would say " Hello, General! How do you do, sir?
Well, I am here to inform you that I am on the
ground, here in the enemy's country, with my regiment of Texas cavalry, eleven hundred strong, well
mounted and armed to the teeth with United States
holster pistols, a good many chop knives, and several
double-barreled shotguns. Send Lyons word to turn
out his Dutch regulars, Kansas jayhawkers and Missouri home guards, and we'll clean 'em up and drive
'em from the State of Missouri."

" Very well, very well, Colonel; go back and order
your men to cook up three days' rations, get all the
ammunition they can scrape up in the neighborhood,
and be in their saddles at eleven o'clock to-night,
and I will have them at Dug Springs at daylight

to-morrow morning and turn them loose on the gentlemen you speak of."

Any way, whatever the interview was, we had
barely stretched out our weary limbs and folded
our arms to sleep when the sergeant-major, that fellow that so often brings bad news, came tripping
along through the encampment, hurrying from one
company's headquarters to another, saying: "Captain, it's General McCulloch's order that you have
your men cook up three days' rations, distribute all
the ammunition they can get and be in their saddles,
ready to march on the enemy, at eleven o'clock to-
night."

Sleep? Oh, no! Where's the man who said he
was sleepy? Cook three days' rations? Oh, my!
And not a cooking vessel in the regiment! But
never mind about that, it's a soldier's duty to obey
orders without asking questions. I drew and distributed the flour and meat, and left the men to do
the cooking while I looked after the ammunition.
Here the men learned to roll out biscuit dough about
the size and shape of a snake, coil it around a ramrod or a small wooden stick, and bake it before the
fire.

This Sunday afternoon and night, August 4, was
a busy time in our camp. Some were cooking the
rations, some writing letters, some one thing, and
some another; all were busy until orders came to
saddle up. We were camped on the main Springfield road, and General Lyon, with his army, was
at Dug Springs, a few miles farther up the same
road. We were to march at eleven o'clock and attack him at daylight Monday morning. There al-

ready had been some skirmishing between our outposts and his scouts. We had never been in battle,
and we were nervous, restless, sleepless for the remainder of the day and night after receiving the
orders.

Some of the things that occurred during the afternoon and night would have been ludicrous had
not the whole occasion been so serious. In my efforts
to obtain and distribute all the ammunition I could
procure I was around among the men from mess
to mess during all this busy time. Scores of letters
were being written by firelight to loved ones at
home, said letters running something like this:

CAMP ————, Mo., Aug. 4, 1861.
My Dear ————:

We arrived at General McCulloch's headquarters
about 10 A. M. to-day, tired, dusty, hungry, and
sleepy, after a long, forced march from Fort Smith,
Ark. We are now preparing for our first battle.
We are under orders to march at eleven o'clock to
attack General Lyon's army at daylight in the
morning. All the boys are busy cooking up three
days' rations. I am very well. If I survive to-morrow's battle I will write a postscript, giving you
the result. Otherwise this will be mailed to you as
it is.

Yours affectionately,

————   ————

Numbers of the boys said to me: " Now, Barron,
if I am killed to-morrow please mail this letter for
me." One said: " Barron, here is my gold watch.

Take it, and if I am killed to-morrow please send it to my mother." Another said: " Barron, here is a gold ring. Please take care of it, and if I am killed to-morrow I want you to send it to my sister." Another one said: " Barron, if I am killed to-morrow I want you to send this back to my father." At last it became funny to me that each seemed to believe in the probability of his being killed the next day, and were making nuncupative wills, naming me as executor in every case, without seeming to think of the possibility of *my* being killed.

During the remainder of our four years' service, with all the fighting we had to do, I never again witnessed similar preparations for battle.

CHAPTER III

OUR FIRST BATTLE

On the March—Little York Raid—Under Fire—Our First
Battle—Oak Hill (Wilson's Creek)—Death of General Lyon—
Our First Charge—Enemy Retires—Impressions of First Bat-
tle—Death of Young Willie—Horrors of a Battlefield—Troops
Engaged—Casualties.

WELL, eleven o'clock came, we mounted our horses
and rode out on the road to Dug Springs, under
orders to move very quietly, and to observe the
strictest silence—and, when necessary, we were not
even to talk above a whisper. The night was dark
and we moved very slowly. About three o'clock in
the morning an orderly came down the column carrying a long sheet of white muslin, tearing off narrow strips, and handing them to the men, one of
which each man was required to tie around his left
arm. From our slow, silent movement I felt as if
we were in a funeral procession, and the white sheet
reminded me of a winding sheet for the dead. As
we were not uniformed these strips were intended as
a mark of the Confederate soldiers, so we might
avoid killing our own men in the heat and confusion
of battle.

At daylight we were halted and informed that
General Lyon's forces had withdrawn from Dug
Springs. After some little delay our army moved
on in the direction of Springfield, infantry and artillery in the road and the cavalry on the flank,—

that is, we horsemen took the brush and marched
parallel with the road, in order to guard against
ambush and surprises. We moved slowly in this
manner nearly all day without coming up with the
enemy—at noon we took a short rest, and dinner,
and here many of us consumed the last of our three
days' rations.

Along in the afternoon, as we were considerably
ahead of the infantry, we filed into the road and
were moving slowly along, when suddenly we heard
firing in our rear. Of course every one supposed the
infantry had come up with the enemy and they were
fighting. We were immediately halted, and Lieutenant-Colonel Lane came galloping back down the
column shouting, "Turn your horses around, men,
and go like h———l the other way." Instantly the
column was reversed, and the next minute we were
following Colonel Lane at full speed. For two or
three miles we ran our tired horses down the dusty
road, only to learn that some of the infantry, who
had stopped to camp, were firing off their guns sim-
ply to unload them.

We then retraced our steps and moved on up the
road to Wilson's Creek, nine miles from Springfield,
and camped on the ground that was to be our first
battlefield. We came to the premises of a Mr.
Sharp, situated on the right hand or east side of
the road. Just beyond his house, down the hill,
the creek crossed the road and ran down through his
place, back of his house and lot. On the left hand
or west side of the road were rough hills covered
with black jack trees, rocks, and considerable un-
derbrush. Before coming to his dwelling we passed

through his lot gates down in the rear of his barn and premises, and camped in a strip of small timber growing along the creek. In the same enclosure, in front and south of us, was a wide, uncultivated field, with a gradual upgrade all the way to the timber back of the field. Here we lived on our meager rations for several days. In the meantime the whole army then in Missouri, including General Sterling Price's command, was concentrated in the immediate vicinity.

One day during the week we heard that a company of Missouri home guards, well armed, were at Little York, a small village six or seven miles west from our camps. Now, the home guards were Northern sympathizers, so one afternoon our company and another of the regiment, by permission, marched to Little York on a raid, intending to capture the company and secure their arms. We charged into the town, but the enemy we sought was not there, and we could find but four or five supposed members of the company. Anyway, we chased and captured every man in town who ran from us, including the surgeon of the command, who was mounted on a good horse, being the only man mounted in the company. Several of the boys had a chase after him, capturing his horse, which was awarded to John B. Long, who, however, did not enjoy his ownership very long, for the animal was killed in our first battle. We then searched for arms, but found none.

In one of the storehouses we found a large lot of pig lead, estimated at 15,000 pounds. This we confiscated for the use of the Confederate Army.

In order to move it, we pressed into service the only
two wagons we could find with teams, but so over-
loaded one of them that the wheels broke down when
we started off.   We then carried the lead on our
horses,—except what we thought could be hauled
in the remaining wagon,—out some distance and
hid it in a thicket of hazelnut bushes.   We then,
with our prisoners and the one wagon, returned to
camp.   When the prisoners were marched up to
regimental   headquarters   Lieutenant-Colonel   Lane
said, " Turn them out of the lines and let them go.
I would rather fight them than feed them."

This raiding party of two companies that made
the descent upon Little York was commanded by
Captain Taylor, and the raid resulted, substantially,
as I have stated.   Nevertheless, even the next day
wild, exaggerated stories of the affair were told, and
believed by many members of our own regiment as
well as other portions of the army, and in Victor
Rose's " History of Ross's Brigade," the following
version of the little exploit may be read: " Captain
Frank Taylor, of Company C, made a gallant dash
into a detachment guarding a train loaded with supplies for Lyon, routing the detachment, taking a
number of prisoners, and capturing the entire
train."   And " the historian " was a member of
Company A, Third Texas Cavalry!   From this language one would infer that Captain Taylor, alone
and unaided, had captured a supply train with its
escort!

On Friday, August 9, the determination was
reached to move on Springfield and attack General
Lyon.   We received orders to cook rations, have

our horses saddled and be ready to march at nine
o'clock P. M.   At nine o'clock we were ready to
mount, but by this time a slight rain was falling,
and the night was very dark and threatening.   We
" stood to horse," as it were, all night, waiting for
orders that never came.   The infantry, also under
similar orders, slept on their arms.   Of course our
men, becoming weary with standing and waiting,
lay down at the feet of their horses, reins in hand,
and slept.   Daylight found some of the men up,
starting little fires to prepare coffee for breakfast,
while the majority were sleeping on the ground, and
numbers of our horses, having slipped their reins
from the hands of the sleeping soldiers, were grazing
in the field in front of the camp.

Captain Taylor had ridden up to regimental headquarters to ask for instructions or orders, when the
enemy opened fire upon us with a battery stationed
in the timber just back of the field in our front, and
the shells came crashing through the small timber
above our heads.   And as if this were a signal, almost instantly another battery opened fire on General Price's camp.   Who was responsible for the
blunder that made it possible for us to be thus surprised in camp, I cannot say.   It was said that
the pickets were ordered in, in view of our moving,
at nine o'clock the night before, and were not sent
out again; but this was afterwards denied.   If we
had any pickets on duty they were certainly very
inefficient.   But there is no time now to inquire of
the whys and wherefores.

Captain Taylor now came galloping back, shouting: " Mount your horses and get into line! "

There was a hustling for loose horses, a rapid mounting and very soon the regiment was in line by companies in the open field in front of the camps. It was my duty now to " form the company," the same as if we were going out to drill; that is, beginning on the right, I rode down the line requiring each man to call out his number, counting, one, two, three, four; one, two, three, four, until the left was reached. This gave every man his place for the day, and every man was required to keep his place. If ordered to march by twos, the horses were wheeled to the right, number 2 forming on the right of number 1; if order to for fours, numbers 3 and 4 moved rapidly up on the right of numbers 1 and 2, and so on. This being done in the face of the aforesaid battery, with no undue haste, was quite a trying ordeal to new troops who had never before been under fire, but the men stood it admirably.

As soon as we were formed we moved out by twos, with orders to cross the Springfield road to the hills beyond, where General Ben McCulloch's infantry, consisting of the noble Third Louisiana and the Arkansas troops, some three thousand in all, were hotly engaged with General Lyon's command. General Lyon was personally in front of General Sterling Price's army of Missouri State Guards, being personally in command of one wing of the Federal Army (three brigades), and Sigel, who was senior colonel, commanded the other wing (one brigade). General McCulloch was in command of the Confederate troops and General Price of the Missourians.

We moved out through Mr. Sharp's premises as

we had come in, but coming to the road we were delayed by the moving trains and the hundreds of unarmed men who were along with General Price's army, rushing in great haste from the battlefield. The road being so completely filled with the mass of moving trains and men rushing pell-mell southward, it cost us a heroic effort to make our way across. In this movement the rear battalion of the regiment, under Major Chilton, was cut off from us, and while they performed good service during part of the day, we saw no more of them until the battle ended.

By the time we crossed the road the battle had become general, and the fire of both artillery and musketry was constant and terrific. The morning was bright and clear and the weather excessively warm, and as we had been rushed into battle without having time to get breakfast or to fill our canteens, we consequently suffered from both hunger and thirst. After crossing the road we moved up just in the rear of our line of infantry, and for five hours or more were thus held in reserve, slowly moving up in column as the infantry lines surged to the left, while the brave Louisiana and Arkansas troops stood their ground manfully against the heavy fire of musketry and artillery. As our position was farther down the hill than that occupied by the line of infantry, we were in no very great danger, as the enemy's shot and shell usually passed over us, but, nevertheless, during the whole time the shots were passing very unpleasantly near our heads, with some damage, too, as a number of the men were wounded about the head. One member of Company

C was clipped across the back of the neck with a
minie ball. After hours of a most stubborn contest
our infantry showed some signs of wavering. Colonel Greer at this critical moment led us up rapidly
past their extreme left,—had us wheel into line, and
then ordered us to charge the enemy's infantry in
our front. With a yell all along the line, a yell
largely mixed with the Indian warwhoop, we dashed
down that rough, rocky hillside at a full gallop
right into the face of that solid line of well-armed
and disciplined infantry. It was evidently a great
surprise to them, for though they emptied their
guns at us, we moved so rapidly that they had no
time to reload, and broke their lines and fled in confusion. The battery that had been playing on our
infantry all day was now suddenly turned upon us,
otherwise we could have ridden their infantry down
and killed or captured many of them, but we were
halted, and moved out by the left flank from under
the fire of their battery. Their guns were now lim-
bered up and moved off, and their whole command
was soon in full retreat towards Springfield. During the engagement General Nathaniel Lyon had
been killed, and the battle, after about seven hours'
hard fighting, was at an end. The field was ours.

Thus ended our first battle. Would to God it
had been our last, and the last of the war! General
McCulloch called it " The Battle of Oak Hill." but
the Federals called it " The Battle of Wilson's
Creek."

This first battle was interesting to me in many
ways. I had been reading of them since my childhood and looking at pictures of battlefields during

and after the conflict, but to see a battle in progress, to hear the deafening roar of artillery, and the terrible, ceaseless rattle of musketry; to see the rapid movements of troops, hear the shouts of men engaged in mortal combat, and to realize the sensation of being a participant, and then after hours of doubtful contest to see the enemy fleeing from the field—all this was grand and terrible. But while there is a grandeur in a battle, there are many horrors, and unfortunately the horrors are wide-spread —they go home to the wives, fathers, mothers, and sisters of the slain.

After the battle was over we were slowly moving in column across the field unmolested, but being fired on by some of the enemy's sharpshooters, who were keeping up a desultory fire at long range, when young Mr. Willie, son of Judge A. H. Willie, a member of Company A, which was in advance of us, came riding up the column, passing us. I was riding with Captain Taylor at the head of our company, and just as Willie was passing us a ball from one of the sharpshooters' rifles struck him in the left temple, and killed him. But for his position the ball would have struck me in another instant.

After all the Federals capable of locomotion had left the field, we were moved up the road on which Sigel had retreated, as far as a mill some five miles away, where we had ample witness of the execution done by our cavalry—dead men in blue were strewn along the road in a horrible manner. On returning, late in the afternoon, we were ordered back to the camp we had left in the morning. As we had wit-

nessed the grandeur of the battle, Felps and myself concluded to ride over the field and see some of
its horrors. So we rode leisurely over the field and
reviewed the numerous dead, both men and horses,
and the few wounded who had not been carried to
the field hospitals. General Lyon's body had been
placed in an ambulance by order of General McCulloch, and was on its way to Springfield, where it
was left at the house of Colonel Phelps. His horse
lay dead on the field, and every lock of his gray
mane and tail was clipped off by our men and carried off as souvenirs.

Further on we found one poor old Missouri home
guard who was wounded. He had dragged himself
up against a black jack tree and was waiting patiently for some chance of being cared for. We
halted and were speaking to him, when one of his
neighbors, a Southern sympathizer, came up, recognized him and began to abuse him in a shameful
manner. "Oh, you d——d old scoundrel," he said,
"if you had been where you ought to have been,
you wouldn't be in the fix you are in now." They
were both elderly men, and evidently lived only a
few miles away, as the Southerner had had time to
come from his home to see the result of the battle.
I felt tempted to shoot the old coward, and thus put
them on an equality, and let them quarrel it out.
But as it seemed enough men had been shot for one
day, we could only shame him and tell him that if he
had had the manliness to take up his gun and fight
for what he thought was right, as his neighbor had
done, he would not be there to curse and abuse a
helpless and wounded man, and that he should not

insult him or abuse him any more while we were there. We continued our ride until satisfied for that time, and for all time, so far as I was concerned, with viewing a battlefield just after the battle, unless duty demands it.

Our train came up at night, bringing us, oh, so many letters from our post office at Fort Smith, but the day's doings, the fatigue, hunger, thirst, heat, and excitement had overcome me so completely that I opened not a letter until the morning. Reckoning up the day's casualties in Company C, we found four men and fifteen horses had been shot; Leander W. Cole was mortally wounded, and died in Springfield a few days later; J. E. Dillard was shot in the leg and in allusion to his long-leggedness it was said he was shot two and one half feet below the knee and one and one half feet above the ankle; T. Wiley Roberts was slightly wounded in the back of the head, and P. C. Coupland slightly wounded. Some of the horses were killed and others wounded. Roger Q. Mills and Dr. —— Malloy, two citizens of Corsicana, were with us in this battle, having overtaken us on the march, and remained with us until it was over, then returning home. Roger Q. Mills was afterwards colonel of the Tenth Texas Infantry. Dr. Malloy was captain of a company, and fell while gallantly fighting at the head of his company in one of the battles west of the Mississippi River.

I will not attempt to give the number of troops engaged, as the official reports of the battle written by the officers in command fail to settle that question. General Price reported that he had 5221 effective men with 15 pieces of artillery. General McCulloch's brigade has been estimated at 4000 men, with no artillery, and this officer's conclusion was that the enemy had 9000 to 10,000 men, and that the forces of the two armies were about equal. The Federal officers in their reports greatly exaggerated our strength, and, I think, greatly underestimated theirs, especially so since, General Lyon being killed, it devolved upon the subordinates to make the reports. Major S. D. Sturgis, who commanded one of Lyon's brigades, says their 3700 men attacked an army of 23,000 rebels under Price and McCulloch, that their loss in killed, wounded, and missing was 1235, and he supposed the rebel loss was 3000. Major J. M. Schofield, General Lyon's adjutant, says their 5000 men attacked the rebel army of 20,000. General Frémont, afterwards, in congratulating the army on their splendid conduct in this battle, says their 4300 men met the rebel army of 20,000. They give the organization of their army without giving the numbers. General Lyon had four brigades, consisting, as they report, of six regiments, three battalions, seven companies, 200 Missouri home guards and three batteries of artillery, many of their troops being regulars. Their army came against us in two columns. General Lyon, with three brigades and two batteries, Totten's six pieces, and Dubois, with four, came down the Springfield road and attacked our main army in front. Colonel Franz Sigel, with one brigade and one light battery, marched down to the left, or east of the road and into our rear, and attacked the cavalry camp with his artillery, as has already been stated.

LIEUTENANT-COLONEL JILES S. BOGGESS
Third Texas Cavalry

Poor Sigel! it would be sufficient to describe his disastrous defeat to merely repeat their official reports.
But I would only say that his battery was lost and
his command scattered and driven from the field in
utter confusion and demoralization in the early part
of the day and that it was followed some five miles
by our cavalry and badly cut up, he himself escap-
ing capture narrowly by abandoning his carriage
and colors and taking to a cornfield. It was said
by the Federals that he reached Springfield with one
man before the battle was ended. But the forces
led by the brave and gallant Lyon fought bravely.
The losses are given officially as follows: Federals:
killed, 223; wounded, 721; missing, 291. Total,
1235. Confederates: killed, 265; wounded, 800;
missing, 30. Total, 1095.

CHAPTER IV

THE WAR IN MISSOURI

Personal Characteristics—Two Braggarts—Joe Welch—
William Hood—We Enter Springfield—Bitter Feeling in Missouri—Company Elections—Measles and Typhoid—Carthage,
and My Illness There—We Leave Carthage—Death of Captain
Taylor—Winter Quarters—Furloughed—Home Again.

A BATTLE—or danger—will often develop some
characteristics that nothing else will bring out.

One Gum was a shabby little man, mounted on
a shabby little mustang pony; in fact his horse was
so shabby that he would tie him, while we were at
Dallas, away off in the brush in a ravine and carry
his forage half a mile to feed him rather than have
him laughed at. Gum was a Missourian, and got
into the company somehow, with his fiddle, and aside
from his fiddling he was of little use in camps.
During the time we were kept slowly moving along
in the rear of our infantry, engaged mainly in the
unprofitable business of dodging balls and shells
that were constantly whizzing near our heads, Captain Taylor was very anxious that his company
should act well under fire and would frequently
glance back, saying: "Keep your places, men."
Gum, however, was out of place so often he finally
became personal, "Keep in your place, Gum." At
this Gum broke ranks and came trotting up on
his little pony, looking like a monkey with a red
cap on, for, having lost his hat, he had tied a red

cotton handkerchief around his head. When opposite the captain he reined up, and with a trembling frame and in a quivering voice, almost crying, he said: "Captain, I *can't* keep my place. I am a coward, and I can't help it." Captain Taylor said, sympathetically: "Very well, Gum; go where you please." It so happened that a few days later we passed his father's house, near Mount Vernon, and the captain allowed him to stop and remain with his father. And thus he was discharged. At this stage of the war we had no army regulations, no "red tape" in our business. If a captain saw fit to discharge one of his men he told him to go, and he went without reference to army headquarters or the War Department. I met Gum in November, fleeing from the wrath of the home guards, as a man who had been in the Confederate Army could not live in safety in Missouri.

One of our men, in the morning when I was forming the company, was so agitated that it was a difficult matter to get him to call his number. During the day a ball cut a gash about skin deep and two inches in length across the back of his neck, just at the edge of his hair. As a result of this we were two years in getting this man under fire again, though he would not make an honest confession like Gum, but would manage in some mysterious way to keep out of danger. When at last we succeeded in getting him in battle at Thompson's Station in 1863, he ran his iron ramrod through the palm of his right hand and went to the rear. Rather than risk himself in another engagement he deserted, in the fall of that year, and went into the Federal breastworks in front of Vicksburg and surrendered. This man was named Wiley Roberts.

Captain Hale, of Company D, was rather rough-hewn, but a brave, patriotic old man, having not the least patience with a thief, a coward, or a braggart. While he had some of the bravest men in his company that any army could boast of, he had one or two, at least, that were not among these, as the two stalwart bullies who were exceedingly boastful of their prowess, of the ease with which Southern men could whip Northerners, five to one being about as little odds as they cared to meet. This type of braggart was no novelty, for every soldier had heard that kind of talk at the beginning of the war. While we were moving out in the morning when Sigel's battery was firing and Captain Hale was coolly riding along at the head of his company, these two men came riding rapidly up, one hand holding their reins while the other was pressed across the stomach, as if they were in great misery, saying, when they sighted their commander: "Captain Hale, where must we go? we are sick." Captain Hale looked around without uttering a word for a moment, his countenance speaking more indignation than language could express. At last he said, in his characteristic, emphatic manner: "Go to h——l, you d——d cowards! You were the only two fighting men I had until now we are in a battle, and you're both sick. I don't care when you go." Other incidents could be given where men in the regiment were tried and found wanting, but the great majority were brave and gallant men who never shirked duty or flinched from danger.

An instance of the opposite character may be told of Joe Welch. Joe was a blacksmith, almost a giant in stature. Roughly guessing, I would say he was six feet two inches in height, weighing about 240 pounds, broad-shouldered, raw-boned, with muscles that would laugh at a sledge. Joe had incurred the contempt of the company by acting in a very cowardly manner, as they thought, in one or two little personal affairs before we reached Missouri. But when we went into battle Joe was there, as unconcerned and cool, apparently, as if he was only going into his shop to do a day's work; and when we made our charge down that rough hillside when the enemy's bullets were coming as thick as hailstones, one of Joe's pistols jolted out of its holster and fell to the ground. Joe reined in his horse, deliberately dismounted, recovered the pistol, remounted, and rapidly moved up to his place in the ranks. Those who witnessed the coolness and apparent disregard of danger with which he performed this little feat felt their contempt suddenly converted into admiration.

Another one of our men was found wanting, but through no fault of his own, as he was faithful as far as able. This was William Hood. Hood was an Englishman, quite small, considerably advanced in years, destitute of physical endurance and totally unfit for the hardships of a soldier's life. He was an old-womanish kind of a man, good for cooking, washing dishes, scouring tin plates, and keeping everything nice around the mess headquarters, but was unsuited for any other part of a soldier's duty. Hood strayed off from us somehow during the day, and for some part of the day was a prisoner, losing his horse, but managed to get back to camp afoot at night, very much depressed in spirits. The next morning he was very proud to discover his horse grazing out in the field two or three hundred yards from the camp. He almost flew to him, but found he was wounded. He came back to Captain Taylor with a very sad countenance, and said: " Captain Taylor, me little 'orse is wounded right were the 'air girth goes on 'im." The wound was only slight and as soon as the little 'orse was in proper traveling condition little Hood was discharged and allowed to return home.

As already stated, we returned late in the evening to the camp we had left in the morning to rest and sleep for the night, for after the excitement of the day was over bodily fatigue was very much in evidence. Our train came up about nightfall, but as I was very tired, and our only chance for lights was in building up little brush fires, the opening of my letters was postponed until the bright Sunday morning, August 11, especially as my mail packet was quite bulky. One large envelope from Huntsville, Ala., contained a letter and an exquisite little Confederate flag some ten or twelve inches long. This was from a valued young lady friend who, in the letter, gave me much good advice, among other things warning me against being shot in the back. And I never was. During the day the command marched into Springfield, to find that the Federal Army had pushed forward Saturday night. They had retreated to Rolla, the terminus of the railroad, and thence returned to St. Louis, leaving us for a long time in undisputed possession of southwest Missouri, where we had but little to do for three months but gather forage and care for our horses and teams and perform the routine duties incident to a permanent camp.

From Springfield we moved out west a few miles, camping for a few days at a large spring called Cave Spring. Here several of our men were discharged and returned home. Among them James R. Taylor, brother of Captain, subsequently Colonel, Taylor of the Seventeenth Texas Cavalry, who was killed at the battle of Mansfield, La.

Southwest Missouri is a splendid country, abounding in rich lands, fine springs of pure water, and this year, 1861, an abundant crop of corn, oats, hay, and such staples had been raised. Nevertheless, a very unhappy state of things existed there during the war, for the population was very much divided in sentiment and sympathy—some being for the North and some for the South, and the antagonism between the factions was very bitter. Indeed, so intense had the feeling run, the man of one side seemed to long to see his neighbor of the other side looted and his property destroyed. Men of Southern sympathy have stealthily crept into our camps at midnight and in whispers told us where some Union men were to be found in the neighborhood, evidently wishing and expecting that we would raid them and kill or capture, rob, plunder or do them damage in some terrible manner. Such reporters seemed to be disappointed when we would tell them that we were not there to make war on citizens, and the Union men themselves seemed to think we were ready to

do violence to all who were not loyal to the Southern
Confederacy.   When we chanced to go to one of
their houses for forage, as frequently happened,
we could never see the man of the house, unless we
caught a glimpse of him as he was running to
some place to hide, and no assurance to his family
that we would not in any manner mistreat him
would overcome the deep conviction that we would.
This bitter feeling and animosity among the citizens grew to such intensity, as the war advanced,
that life became a misery to the citizen of Missouri.

    We moved around leisurely over the country from
place to place, foraging and feeding a few days
here and a few days there, and in the early days of
September, passing by way of Mount Vernon and
Carthage, we found ourselves at Scott's Mill, on
Cowskin River, near the border of the Cherokee
Nation.   At Mount Vernon we witnessed a farce en-
acted by Company D.   Dan Dupree was their first
lieutenant, and a very nice, worthy fellow he was,
too, but some of his men fell out with him about
some trivial matter, and petitioned him to resign,
which he did.   Captain Hale, supposing possibly
they might also be opposed to him, and too diffi-
dent to say so, he resigned too, and the other officers
followed suit, even down to the fourth and last corporal, and for the time the company was without
an officer, either commissioned or non-commissioned.
At this early stage of the war, for an officer to
resign was a very simple and easy thing.   He had
only to say publicly to his company, " I resign,"
and it was so.   The company was now formed into

line to prepare for the election of officers, and the mode of procedure was as follows: The candidates would stand a few paces in front of the line, their back to the men. The men were then instructed to declare their choice, by standing behind him, one behind the other, and when all votes were counted the result was declared. The outcome on this occasion was that Captain Hale and all the old officers were re-elected, except Dupree. Later in the year members of Company A petitioned their captain to resign, but he respectfully declined, and though many of his men were very indignant, we heard no more of petitioning officers to resign.

While we were camped on the beautiful little Cowskin River measles attacked our men, and we moved up to Carthage, where we remained about eight weeks, during which time we passed through a terrible scourge of measles and typhoid fever. As a result Company C lost five men, including Captain Taylor. Fortunately we were in a high, healthy country, and met in Carthage a warm-hearted, generous people. In addition to our competent and efficient surgeon and his assistant during this affliction, we had a number of good physicians, privates in the regiment, who rendered all the assistance in their power in caring for the sick. The court house was appropriated as a hospital, and, soon filled to its capacity, the generous citizens received the sick men into their houses and had them cared for there. How many of the regiment were sick at one time I do not know, but there were a great many; the number of dead I never knew. Our surgeon went from house to house visiting and prescribing for the sick both day and night, until it seemed sometimes as if he could not make another round.

The day after we reached Carthage I was taken down with a severe case of measles, and glided easily into a case of typhoid fever. Dr. McDugald went personally to find a home for me, and had me conveyed to the residence of Mr. John J. Scott, a merchant and farmer, where for seven weeks I wasted away with the fever, during all of which time I was as kindly and tenderly cared for by Mrs. Scott as if I had been one of her family; and her little girl Olympia, then about eleven years old, was as kind and attentive to me as a little sister could have been. My messmate and chum, Thomas J. Johnson, remained with me to wait on me day and night during the entire time, and Dr. McDugald, and also Dr. Dan Shaw, of Rusk County, were unremitting in their attention. A. B. Summers took charge of my horse, and gave him better attention than he did his own. Captain Taylor was also very low at the same time, and was taken care of at the house of Colonel Ward. The fever had left me and I had been able to sit up in a rocking chair by the fire a little while at a time for a few days, when General Frémont, who had been placed in command of the Federal Army in Missouri, began a movement from Springfield in the direction of Fayetteville, Ark., and we were suddenly ordered away from Carthage. All the available transportation had to be used to remove the sick, who were taken to Scott's Mill. A buggy being procured for Captain Taylor and myself, our horses were hitched to it and, with the assistance of Tom Johnson and John A. Boyd, we moved out, following the march of the command into Arkansas. The command moved south, via Neosho and Pineville, and dropped down on Sugar Creek, near Cross Hollows, confronting General Frémont, who soon retired to Springfield, and never returned. At Sugar Creek we stole Ben A. Long out of camp, and made our way to Fayetteville, where we stopped at the house of Martin D. Frazier, by whose family we were most hospitably treated. Here Captain Taylor relapsed, and died.

Captain Francis Marion Taylor was a noble, brave, and patriotic man, and we were all much grieved at his death. He had been at death's door in Carthage, and Dr. McDugald then thought he was going to die, telling him so, but he rallied, and when we left there he was much stronger than I was, being able to drive, while that would have been impossible with me. When he relapsed he did not seem to have much hope of recovering, and after the surgeon, at his own request, had told him his illness would terminate fatally, he talked very freely of his approaching death. He had two little children, a mother, and a mother-in-law, Mrs. Wiggins, all of whom he loved very much, and said he loved his mother-in-law as much as he loved his mother. He gave me messages for them, placed everything he had with him (his horse, gold watch, gold rings, sword, and his trunk of clothes) in my charge, with specific instructions as to whom to give them—his mother, his mother-in-law and his two little children.

I continued to improve, but recovered very slowly indeed, and remained in Fayetteville until the early days of December. The regiment was ordered to go into winter quarters at the mouth of Frog Bayou, on the north bank of the Arkansas River, twelve miles below Van Buren, and when they had passed through Fayetteville on their way to the designated point, I followed, as I was now able to ride on horseback. Cabins were soon erected for the men and stalls for the horses, and here the main command was at home for the winter. I was furloughed until March 1, but as the weather was fine I remained in the camp for two weeks before starting on the long home journey to Rusk. Many other convalescents were furloughed at this time, so finally, in company with Dr. W. L. Gammage, who, by the way, had been made surgeon of an Arkansas regiment, and two or three members of Company F who lived in Cherokee County, I started to Rusk, reaching the end of my journey just before Christmas.

My first night in Cherokee County was spent at the home of Captain Taylor's noble mother, near Larissa, where I delivered her son's last messages to her, and told her of his last days. The next day I went on to Rusk and delivered the messages, horse, watch, etc., to the mother-in-law and children. Mr. Wiggins's family offered me a home for the winter, and as I had greatly improved and the winter was exceedingly mild, I spent the time very pleasantly until ready to return to the army. Among other things I brought home the ball that killed Leander Cole, and sent it to his mother.

CHAPTER V

THE WAR IN MISSOURI—*Continued*

I Rejoin the Command—Sleeping in Snow—Ambushed—
Battle of Elkhorn Tavern (Pea Ridge)—Capturing a Battery
—Deaths of Generals McCulloch and McIntosh—Battle Continued—Casualties—Keetsville—Official Reports—March Southward—Foraging—Lost Artillery—Illness Again.

In the latter part of February, 1862, I left Rusk in company with Tom Hogg, John Germany, and perhaps one or two more of our furloughed men, for our winter quarters on the Arkansas River. We crossed Red River and took the road running along the line between Arkansas and the Indian Territory to Fort Smith. After crossing Red River we began meeting refugees from Missouri and north Arkansas, on their way to Texas, who told us that our army was moving northward, and a battle was expected very soon. This caused us to push on more rapidly, as we were due to return March 1, and were anxious to be in our places with the command. When we reached Van Buren we learned that our whole army was· in motion, that a battle was imminent and might occur any day. By this time the weather had grown quite cold, and leaving Van Buren at 9 A. M., we had to cross Boston Mountain, facing a north wind blowing snow in our faces all day. Nevertheless, we slept fifty miles from there that night, camping with some commissary wagons on the road, a few miles from Fayetteville. Here we learned that the army was

camped along the road between there and Fayetteville. The next morning we started on at a brisk
gait, but before we could pass the infantry they were
filing into the road. We took to the brush and galloped our horses about six miles and overtook the
Third Texas, which was in the advance, now passing out of the northern suburbs of Fayetteville, and
found Company C in the advance guard on the Bentonville road.

We advanced slowly that day, without coming in
contact with the enemy, and camped that night at
Elm Springs, where the snow fell on us all night.
Of course we had no tents, but slept on the ground
without shelter. This seemed pretty tough to a fellow who, except for a few fine days in December,
had not spent a day in camp since September, during all that time occupying warm, comfortable
rooms. Up to this time I had never learned to sleep
with my head covered, but finding it now necessary,
I would first cover my head and face to keep the
snow out, stand that as long as I could, then throw
the blanket off, when the snow would flutter down in
my face, chilling me so that I could not sleep. So
between the two unpleasant conditions I was unable
to get any rest at all. Some time before daybreak
we saddled up and moved on, the snow being three
or four inches deep, and early in the morning we
passed the burning fires of the Federal pickets. By
nine o'clock the storm had passed, the sun shining
brightly, and about ten o'clock we came in sight of
Bentonville, a distance said to be two miles. We
could plainly see the Federal troops moving about
the streets, their bright guns glistening in the sun-

shine, afterwards ascertained to have been Sigel's column of General Curtis' army. We were drawn up in line and ordered to prepare for a charge. To illustrate what a magic influence an order to charge upon the enemy has, how it sends the sluggish blood rushing through the veins and livens up the new forces, I will say that while we were standing in line preparing to charge those fellows, I was so benumbed with cold that I could not cap my pistols. I tried ever so hard to do so, but had my life depended upon it I could not have succeeded. We were thrown into columns of fours and ordered to charge, which we did at a brisk gallop, and before we had gone exceeding one-half mile I had perfect use of my hands, was comfortably warm, and did not suffer in the least with cold at any time during the rest of the day.

We charged into the town, but the enemy had all moved out. I suppose it was the rear of the command that we had seen moving out. That afternoon we were ambushed by a strong force, and were fired on in the right flank from a steep, rough hill. We were ordered to charge, which order we attempted to obey by wheeling and charging in line up a hill so steep and rough that only a goat could have made any progress, only to find our line broken into the utmost confusion and under a murderous fire of infantry and artillery from an invisible enemy behind rocks and trees. In the confusion I recognized the order "dismount and fall into line!" I dismounted, but when I fell into what I supposed was going to be the line I found Lieutenant J. E. Dillard and J. B. Murphy, " us three, and no more." While glancing back I saw the regi-

ment was charging around on horseback, while the
captains of companies were shouting orders to their
men in the vain endeavor to get them into some
kind of shape.

In the meantime the bullets were coming thick
around us three dismounted men, knocking the bark
from the hickory trees in our vicinity into our
faces in a lively manner. Finally concluding we
could do no good without support, we returned to
our horses, mounted, and joined the confusion, and
soon managed to move out of range of the enemy's
guns. Brave old Captain Hale, very much cha-
grined and mortified by this affair, considered the
regiment disgraced, and said as much in very emphatic, but not very choice, English. I do not remember the precise language he used, but he was
quoted as saying: " This here regiment are disgraced forever! I'd 'a' rather died right thar than
to a give airy inch! " I do not know how many men
we lost in this affair, but Vic. Rose says ten killed
and twenty wounded. I remember that Joe Welch
was wounded in the thigh, but I do not remember
any other casualty in Company C. This was reck-
oned as the first day of the three days' battle of Elkhorn Tavern, or Pea Ridge.

General Earl Van Dorn had taken command of
the entire army on March 2, and conducted the remainder of the campaign to its close. General
Price's division consisted of the Missouri troops.
General McCulloch was placed in command of the
infantry of his old division, consisting of the Third
Louisiana, commanded by Colonel Louis Hebert (pro-
nounced Hebair), and the Arkansas infantry, and

General James McIntosh, who had just been promoted to brigadier-general, commanded the cavalry. Brigadier-General Samuel R. Curtis, who commanded the Federal Army in our front, was concentrating his forces near Elkhorn Tavern and Pea Ridge, near the Arkansas and Missouri line.

After the ambush and skirmish alluded to above, General Sigel moved on northward with his command and we moved on in the same direction, and near nightfall camped by the roadside. Here, as we had neither food for man nor forage for beast, I started out to procure a feed of corn for my horse, if possible, riding west from camp, perhaps five miles, before I succeeded. For a while at first I searched corncribs, but finding them all empty I began searching under the beds, and succeeded in obtaining fifteen or twenty ears. Part of this I fed to my horse, part of it I ate myself, and carried part of it on for the next night.

We were now near the enemy. Leaving camp about two hours before daylight, we made a detour to the left, passed the enemy's right flank, and were in his rear near Pea Ridge. General Price, accompanied by General Van Dorn, passed around his left and gained his rear near Elkhorn Tavern, where General Van Dorn established his headquarters. About 10.30 A. M. we heard General Price's guns, as he began the attack. Our cavalry was moving in a southeasterly direction toward the position of General Sigel's command, and near Leetown, in columns of fours, abreast, the Third Texas on the right, then the Sixth and Ninth Texas, Brook's Arkansas battalion, and a battalion of Choctaw Indians, forming in all, five

columns.   Passing slowly through an open field, a
Federal light battery, some five hundred or six hundred yards to our right, supported by the Third
Iowa Cavalry, opened fire upon our flank, killing one
or two of our horses with the first shot.   The battery was in plain view, being inside of a yard surrounding a little log cabin enclosed with a rail fence
three or four feet high.   Just at this time one of
General McCulloch's batteries, passing us on its way
to the front, was halted, the Third Texas was moved
up in front of it, and were ordered to remain and
protect it.   Lieutenant-Colonel Walter P. Lane rode
out to the front, facing the enemy's battery, and
calling to Charley Watts, he said: " Come here,
Charley, and blow the charge until you are black in
the face."   With Watts by his side blowing the
charge with all his might, Lane struck a gallop, when
the other four columns wheeled and followed him, the
Texans yelling in the usual style and the Indians re-
peating the warwhoop, dashing across the field in
handsome style.   The Federal cavalry charged out
and met them, when a brisk fire ensued for a few minutes ; but, scarcely checking their gait, they brushed
the cavalry, the Third Iowa, aside as if it was chaff,
charged on in face of the battery, over the little rail
fence, and were in possession of the guns in less
time than it takes to tell the story.   In this little
affair twenty-five of the Third Iowa Cavalry were
killed and a battery captured, but I do not know
how many of the gunners were killed.   The
Choctaws, true to their instinct, when they found the
dead on the field, began scalping them, but were soon
stopped, as such savagery could not be tolerated in

civilized warfare. Still a great deal was said by the Federal officers and newspapers about the scalping of a few of these men, and it was reported that some bodies were otherwise mutilated. Colonel Cyrus Bussey of the Third Iowa certified that he found twenty-five of his men dead on the field, and that eight of these had been scalped.

General McCulloch's infantry and artillery soon attacked General Sigel's command in our front, and the engagement became general all along the line. The roar of artillery and the rattle of musketry were terrific all day until dark, with no decisive advantage gained on either side. The Third Texas was moved up behind Pea Ridge, dismounted, and placed in line of battle just behind the crest of the ridge, to support our infantry, a few hundred yards in front of us, with orders not to abandon the ridge under any circumstances. Here we remained until late in the afternoon without further orders, in no particular danger except from the shells from the enemy's artillery that came over the ridge and fell around us pretty constantly. Generals McCulloch and McIntosh had both been killed early in the day, and Colonel Louis Hebert, who was senior colonel and next in rank, had been captured. All this was unknown to us, and also unknown to General Van Dorn, who was with General Price near Elkhorn Tavern, two or three miles east of our position. Late in the afternoon Colonel Greer sent a courier in search of General McIntosh or General McCulloch, to ask for instructions, or orders, and the sad tidings came back that they were both killed; nor could Colonel Hebert be found.

The firing ceased at night, but we remained on the field, uncertain as to the proper thing to do, until a courier who had been sent to General Van Dorn returned about 2 A. M., with orders for all the forces to move around to General Price's position.   When this was accomplished it was near daylight, and we had spent the night without sleep, without rations, and without water.   General Curtis, perhaps discovering our movement, was also concentrating his forces in General Price's front.

The Confederates made an attack on the enemy early in the morning, and for an hour or two the firing was brisk and spirited, but as our men were starved out and their ammunition about exhausted, they were ordered to cease firing.   As the Federals also ceased firing, the forces were withdrawn quietly and in an orderly manner from the field, and we moved off to the south, moving east of General Curtis, having passed entirely around his army.

The number of forces engaged in this battle were not definitely given.   General Van Dorn in his report stated that he had less than 14,000 men, and estimated the Federal force at from 17,000 to 24,000, computing our loss at 600 killed and wounded and 200 prisoners, a total of 800.   General Curtis reported that his forces engaged consisted of about 10,500 infantry and cavalry, with 49 pieces of artillery, and his statement of losses, killed, wounded, and missing adds up a total of 1384.   The future historian, the man who is so often spoken of, is going to have a tough time if he undertakes to record the truths of the war.   When commanding officers will give some facts and then round up their official re-

ports with fiction, conflicts will arise that, it appears
to me, can never be reconciled. A private soldier
or a subordinate officer who participates in a battle
can tell little about it beyond what comes under his
personal observation, which is not a great deal, but
he is apt to remember that little very distinctly.

In reference to the close of the battle, General
Curtis among other things said: " Our guns continued some time after the rebel fire ceased and the
rebels had gone down into the deep caverns through
which they had begun their precipitate flight. Finally
our firing ceased." Speaking of the pursuit he says:
" General Sigel also followed in this pursuit towards
Keetsville . . . General Sigel followed some miles
north towards Keetsville, firing on the retreating
force that ran that way." Then adds: " The main
force took the Huntsville road which is directly
south." This is true. Now, I dare say, there never
was a more quiet, orderly, and uninterrupted retreat
from a battlefield. The Third Texas was ordered to
cover the retreat, and in order to do this properly we
took an elevated position on the battlefield, where we
had to remain until our entire army moved off and
everybody else was on the march and out of the way.
The army moved out, not precipitately, but in a
leisurely way, not through " deep caverns," but over
high ground in plain view of the surrounding country. Company C was ordered to take the position
of rear guard, in rear of the regiment. The regiment finally moved out, Company C waiting until
it had gone some distance, when the company filed
into the road and moved off. And then James E.
Dillard and the writer of this remained on the field

until the entire Confederate army was out of sight. During all this time not a Federal gun was fired, not a Federal soldier came in view. Nor were we molested during the entire day or night, although we moved in a leisurely way all day, and at night Company C was on picket duty in the rear until midnight.

Keetsville is a town in Missouri north of the battle-field. Sigel, it was stated, "followed some miles north towards Keetsville, firing on the retreating force that ran that way." There were about twenty-four pieces of our artillery that got into the Keets-ville road through mistake; they were without an escort, entirely unprotected. After we had gone about three days' march, leaving Huntsville to our left and Fayetteville to the right, the Third Texas was sent in search of this artillery, and, after marching all night and until noon next day, passing through Huntsville, we met them, and escorted them in. They had not been fired on or molested in the least. The Federal officers, however, were not chargeable with all the inaccuracies that crept into official reports.

General Van Dorn in his report of this campaign, says: "On the 6th we left Elm Springs for Bentonville. . . . I therefore endeavored to reach Bentonville, eleven miles distant, by rapid march, but the troops moved so slowly that it was 11 A. M. before the leading division (Price's)—reached the village, and we had the mortification to see Sigel's division, 7000 strong, leaving it as we entered."

Now, as I have already stated, the Third Texas was in advance, and we saw Sigel leaving Bentonville long before 11 A. M., and Price's division never saw them in Bentonville nor anywhere else that day. General Curtis reported that two of his divisions had just reached his position, near Pea Ridge, when word came to him that General Sigel, who had been left behind with a detachment of one regiment, was about to be surrounded by a " vastly superior force," when these two divisions marched rapidly back and with infantry and artillery checked the rebel advance, losing twenty-five men killed and wounded. So this was the force that ambushed us, and according to this account, Sigel moved out of Bentonville in the morning with one regiment, instead of 7000 men. So the reader of history will never know just how much of fiction he is getting along with the " history."

Leaving the battlefield in the manner stated, we moved very slowly all day. In fact, fatigue, loss of sleep, and hunger had rendered a rapid movement impossible with the infantry. Our men were so starved that they would have devoured almost anything. During the day I saw some of the infantry men shoot down a hog by the side of the road, and, cutting off pieces of the meat, march on eating the raw bloody pork without bread or salt. The country through which we were marching was a poor, mountainous district, almost destitute of anything for the inhabitants to subsist upon, to say nothing of feeding an army. Stock of any kind appeared to be remarkably scarce. J. E. Dillard managed to get a small razor-back pig, that would weigh perhaps twenty-five pounds, strapped it on behind his saddle and thus carried it all day. When we were relieved of picket duty and went into camp at midnight, he cut it up and divided it among the men. I drew a shoulder-blade, with perhaps as much as four ounces of meat on it. This I broiled and ate without salt or bread.

We continued the march southward, passing ten or twelve miles east of Fayetteville. About the fourth day we had been resting, and the commissary force was out hustling for something to eat, but before we got any rations the Third Texas was suddenly ordered to mount immediately and go in search of our missing artillery. This was in the afternoon, perhaps four o'clock. Moving in a northeasterly direction, we marched all night on to the headwaters of White River, where that stream is a mere creek, and I do not think it would be an exaggeration to say that we crossed it twenty times during the night. About 10 A. M. we passed through Huntsville, county seat of Madison County, a small town having the appearance of being destitute of everything. By this time the matter of food had become a very serious question, and we appeared to be in much greater danger of dying from starvation in the mountains of northern Arkansas than by the enemy's bullets. Our belts had been tightened until there was no relief in that, and, as if to enhance my own personal suffering, the tantalizing fact occurred to me that I was treading my native heath, so to speak, for I am a native of Madison County, and Huntsville had been my home for years, where to enjoy three squares a day had been an unbroken habit of years. But to-day I was literally starving in the town of Huntsville, County of Madison, aforesaid, and not a friendly face could I see, nor could a morsel of bread be procured for love or patriotism. Passing onward two or three miles, and having learned that the guns were coming, we rested, and privately made details to scour the country and beg for a little food " for sick and wounded men." Tom Johnson went out for our mess, and the sorrowful tales that were told in behalf of the poor sick and wounded soldiers we were hauling along in ambulances, with nothing with which to feed them, would have melted a heart of stone. The ruse was a success, as the details came in at night with divers small contributions made from scant stores for " the poor sick and wounded men," which were ravenously consumed by the well ones. The artillery shortly afterwards came up and was escorted by us to the command. Camping that night a few miles from Huntsville, the artillery had taken the wrong road as it left the battlefield, had gone up into Missouri, and had had a long circuitous drive through the mountains, but otherwise they were all right.

After we returned with the guns, the army moved on southward. When we were again in motion, as there was no further apprehension of being followed by the enemy, hunger having nearly destroyed my respect for discipline, I left the column by a by-road leading eastwardly, determined to find something to eat. This proved a more difficult errand than I had expected, for the mountaineers were very poor and apparently almost destitute of supplies. I had traveled twelve or fifteen miles when I rode down the mountain into a little valley, at the head of Frog Bayou, coming to a good log house owned and occupied by a Mr. Jones, formerly of Jackson County, Alabama, and a brother of Hosea, Allen, William, and Jesse Jones, good and true men, all of whom I knew. If he had been my uncle I could not have been prouder to find him. Here I got a good square meal for myself and horse, seasoned with a good hearty welcome. This good, true old man was afterwards murdered, as I learned, for his loyalty to the Confederate cause. After enjoying my dinner and a rest, I proceeded on my way, intending to rejoin the command that evening; but, missing the road they were on, I met the regiment at our old winter quarters. Thus about the middle of March the Third Texas Cavalry was again housed in the huts we had erected on the bank of the Arkansas River. I do not know the casualties of the regiment, but as far as I remember Company C had only one man, Jos. Welsh, wounded, and one man, Orderly Sergeant W. M. Caldwell, captured. But as the prisoners were exchanged, our captured men soon returned to us.

Thus ended a short campaign which involved much suffering to me, as well as others, and was the beginning of trouble which nearly cost me my life, a trouble which was not fully recovered from until the following winter. When I was taken with measles in Missouri, the disease affected my bowels, and they became ulcerated, and all through the long spell of typhoid fever and the very slow convalescence this trouble was very hard to control. When I left Rusk to return to the army I was apparently well, but having been comfortably housed all winter was not in proper condition to enter such a campaign at this

CAPTAIN D. R. GURLEY
Sixth Texas Cavalry, A. A. G. Ross' Brigade

season of the year. Before leaving winter quarters the men were ordered to prepare ten days' rations, and when we overtook the command at Fayetteville they had been out nearly that length of time, and rations were already growing scarce. We furloughed men and a number of recruits who had accompanied us to join the command were not here to draw or prepare rations, and our only chance for a living was to share rations with our comrades, who were as liberal and generous as they could be, but they were not able to do much.

From the time I overtook the command until we got back to winter quarters was about ten days, and the few days we were in winter quarters were spent in preparing to cross the Mississippi River. For the first four or five days I managed to procure, on an average, about one biscuit per day; for the other five days we were fortunate to get anything at all to eat, and usually got nothing. We were in the snow for two days and nights, and in a cold, drenching rain one night. On the 7th it was impossible to get a drink of water, to say nothing of food and sleep, and from the time the firing began in the morning until the next morning we could get no water, although we were intensely thirsty. While at winter quarters I had a chill, and started down grade in health, a decline in physical condition that continued until I was apparently nearly dead.

In December parts of our cavalry regiments went with Colonel James McIntosh into the Indian Territory to suppress Hopothlaohola, an ex-chief of the Creek nation, who, with a considerable band of disaffected followers, was making trouble, and part

of the Third Texas went on this expedition.   They
had a battle with the Indians in the mountains on
the headwaters of Chustenala Creek, defeated and
scattered the warriors, captured their squaws, ponies,
and negroes, scattering them so effectually that we
had no further trouble with them.

CHAPTER VI

THE SIEGE OF CORINTH

Leaving Winter Quarters—The Prairies—Duvall's Bluff—
Awaiting Transportation—White River—The Mississippi—
Memphis—Am Detailed—En Route to Corinth—Corinth—Red
Tape—Siege of Corinth—"A Soldier's Grave"—Digging for
Water—Suffering and Sickness—Regiment Reorganized—
Evacuation of Corinth.

CAPTAIN FRANK M. TAYLOR having died, First Lieutenant J. J. A. Barker was promoted to captain and
Private James E. Dillard was promoted to second
lieutenant. After remaining at our winter quarters
for a few days, resting and feeding up, we started on
our long eastward journey, leaving the wounded and
sick in charge of Dr. I. K. Frazer. We moved down
on the north side of the Arkansas River, stopping
two or three days opposite Little Rock. During our
stay here I availed myself of the opportunity of
seeing the capital of the State. From Little Rock
we crossed the country to Duvall's Bluff on White
River, where the men were requested to dismount,
send their horses back to Texas, and go afoot for a
time. This they agreed to without a murmur, on
the promise that, at a proper time, we should be remounted.

On this march from Arkansas River to White
River we crossed grand prairie, and, though I had
often heard of these great stretches of dead level
country, had never seen them. I do not know the

distance that we marched in this grand prairie, but it was a good many miles, as we entered it early in the morning one day and had to camp in it that night, and for almost the whole distance water stood on the ground to the depth of about two or three inches, and it was a difficult matter to find dry ground enough to camp on at night.

Men having been detailed to take our horses back to Texas, the animals were prepared for the journey, each detailed man having to manage a number of horses; and to do this they tied the reins of one horse to the tail of another, each man riding one horse and guiding the leader of the others, strung out in pairs behind him. As they were recrossing the grand prairie the buffalo-gnats attacked the horses, stampeding them and scattering them for many miles over the country, and were with much difficulty recaptured.

We waited several days at Duvall's Bluff for transportation to Memphis, Tenn., on our way to Corinth, Miss. General Joseph L. Hogg, who had been commissioned brigadier-general, accompanied by his staff, came to us here, with orders to take command of a brigade, including the Third Texas Cavalry at Memphis. General Hogg's staff was composed of civilians who had never seen service in the army, and this proved to be an unfortunate time of the year for men not inured to camp life to go into active service. His staff consisted of William T. Long, quartermaster; Daniel P. Irby, commissary; H. H. Rogers, of Jefferson, usually called General Rogers, ordnance officer; in addition there were E. C. Williams, John T. Decherd, and H. S. Newland.

After several days' waiting a steamboat came up the river, landing at the Bluff, and we were crowded upon it for our journey down White River into the Mississippi and up to Memphis, and it was hard to realize that the booming, navigable river we were now on was the same stream we had forded so many times in the mountains of northern Arkansas on the night we went in search of our lost artillery. When we got on the Mississippi we found it very high, numbers of houses along the banks being surrounded by water up to the front doorsteps, where numerous small skiffs could be seen moored. These skiffs furnished the residents their only means of going from house to house.

Arriving at Memphis, we marched away up Poplar Street to the suburbs, and camped in a grove, where we remained several days, spending the time in preparation for the move to Corinth, Miss. Here General Hogg took formal command of his brigade, and, having told me that he wanted Tom Johnson and myself at his headquarters, he had us detailed,—Tom to the ordnance department and me in the quartermaster's department, while John A. Boyd was detailed to work in the commissary department.

Word having finally come for us to proceed to Corinth, we were crowded into a train on the Memphis & Charleston Railroad, en route to that city. On this train, as conductor, I found my former friend and schoolmate, William Wingo. The trip to Corinth was a very slow and tedious one, the train being loaded down with troops and supplies, and unfortunately had lost so much time it had to be run very carefully and make numerous stops. In con-

sequence of this, some of our over-suspicious " pa-
triots " went to General Hogg and implied that the
enemy had forces but a short distance north of us
and that the slow running and the many stoppages
of the train was done evidently through treachery,
and that the plan apparently was to give the enemy
an opportunity to capture the train with the men
and munitions on board.

I had been riding on a rear platform, conversing
with Mr. Wingo, when I proceeded to General
Hogg's coach, and found him considerably excited.
In answer to my inquiry he told me what had been
intimated and said the suggestion, he thought, was
a plausible one, and that he had about determined
to order the train forward at all hazards.   He was
rather an irritable man, and his suspicions were easily
aroused.   I endeavored to quiet him, and did so for
a time, by explaining the situation, and pointed out
the danger we would be in of colliding with some
other train unless the utmost caution was used, as
was being done ; and finally told him that I had
known the conductor since he was a small boy, had
gone to school with him, and was sure there was no
treachery in him.   It was not a great while, however,
before others came around with similar evil suspicions, until the general was wrought up to such a
pitch that he peremptorily ordered the train run
through to Corinth, regardless of consequences, else
some dire calamity would overtake every person in
charge of it.   Well, we made the rest of the journey
in very good time, at the risk of many lives, but fortunately without accident.   For this our friend and
new brigadier-general was on the next day ordered

under arrest by General Beauregard.   But nothing more ever came of it.

After dragging along for more than thirty hours over a distance ordinarily made in six or seven, we finally disembarked, in the middle of the night, on the north side of the railroad, about two miles west of Corinth.   So here we were, without horses, to confront new conditions, under new commanders, constrained to learn the art of war in a different arm of the service, and to drill, to march, and fight as infantry.

The next morning after our arrival I mounted the quartermaster's horse, and rode into town, which was my duty as the quartermaster's right-hand man, to procure forage for our stock—that is, for the regimental and brigade headquarters horses, artillery horses and the wagon teams.   I found the road leading from our camp to town almost impassable owing to the mud, impassable even for a good horse and rider, and utterly and absolutely impassable for a wagon at all, as the best team we had could not have drawn an empty wagon over the road.

I found Corinth all aglitter with brass buttons and gold lace, the beautiful Confederate uniform being much in evidence everywhere.   I never had seen anything like it before.

The Battle of Shiloh had been fought while we were on the steamer between Duvall's Bluff and Memphis, General Albert Sidney Johnston had been killed, and the army under General Beauregard had fallen back to Corinth, and the town was literally alive with officers and soldiers.   There were more headquarters, more sentinels, and more red tape here than I had ever dreamed of. I had not seen uniformed officers or men west of the Mississippi River, and had known nothing of red tape in the army. Knowing nothing of the organization of the army beyond our own brigade, I had everything to learn in reference to the proper quartermaster, forage master, and master of transportation, as I must needs have railroad transportation for my forage.

So beginning at the top, I made my way to General Beauregard's headquarters; from there I was directed to division headquarters; thence to a quartermaster; and from one quartermaster to another, until I had about done the town—and finally found the right man. One lesson learned not to be gone over. Finding there was no difficulty in getting forage delivered in Corinth, I had now to hunt up the master of transportation and satisfy him of the impossibility of hauling it on wagons. Owing to the immense business just then crowding the railroad and the scarcity of rolling stock, it was really a difficult matter to get the transportation; but by dint of perseverance in the best persuasive efforts I could bring to bear, I succeeded in having one day's rations sent out by rail. The next day the same thing as to transportation had to be gone over, and the next, and the next, and each succeeding day it became more difficult to accomplish, until a day came when it was impossible to get the forage hauled out at all.

I rode back to camp and notified the battery and the different headquarters that I would issue forage in Corinth, which would have to be brought out on horseback. All accepted the situation cheerfully except Rogers, who didn't seem to like me, and I suppose it was because I called him *Mr*. Rogers, instead of General Rogers, as others did. He went directly to General Hogg and said: " I think that fellow Barron should be required to have the forage hauled out." General Hogg said: " I do not think you should say a word, sir; you have been trying for a week to get a carload of ammunition brought out and have failed. This is the first day Barron has failed to get the forage brought out; if you want your horses to have corn, ·send your servant in after it." I had no further trouble with Mr. Rogers.

I cannot remember exactly the time we spent at Corinth. It was from the time of our landing there until about the 29th day of May, say six or seven weeks; but to measure time by the suffering and indescribable horrors of that never-to-be-forgotten siege, it would seem not less than six or seven months. From the effects of malaria, bad water, and other combinations of disease-producing causes, our friends from home soon began to fall sick, and, becoming discouraged, the staff officers began to resign and leave the service. Rogers, I believe, was the first to go. He was soon followed by the quartermaster and commissary, and soon all the gentlemen named as coming to the front with General Hogg were gone, except John T. Decherd, who had been made quartermaster in place of William T. Long, resigned. I bought Long's horse and rigging, and Decherd and myself continued to run that department for a time, and Tom Johnson was made ordnance officer in place of Rogers, resigned. General Hogg, being stricken down with disease, was removed to the house of a citizen two or three miles in the country, where he was nursed by his faithful servant Bob, General W. L. Cabell meantime being placed in command of the brigade. General Hogg died a few days later—on the day of the battle of Farmington.

The following "pathetic story of Civil War times" having been published in the Nashville (Tenn.) *Banner, Youth's Companion*, Jacksonville (Tex.) *Reformer*, and perhaps many other papers, I insert it here in order to give its correction a sort of permanent standing:

A SOLDIER'S GRAVE

A pathetic story of Civil War times is related to the older people of Chester County in the western part of Tennessee by the recent death of ex-Governor James S. Hogg of Texas. Some days after the battle of Shiloh, one of the decisive and bloody engagements of the war, fought on April 6-7, 1862, a lone and wounded Confederate soldier made his way to a log cabin located in the woods four miles west of Corinth, Miss., and begged for shelter and food. The man was weak from hunger and loss of blood, and had evidently been wandering through the woods of the sparsely settled section for several days after the battle. The occupants of the cottage had little to give, but divided this little with the soldier. They took the man in and administered to his wants as best they could with their limited resources. They were unable to secure medical attention, and the soldier, already emaciated from the lack of food and proper attention, gradually grew weaker and weaker until he died. Realizing his approaching end, the soldier requested that his body be buried in the wood near the house, and marked with a simple slab bearing his name, " General J. L. Hogg, Rusk, Texas."

The request was complied with, and in the years that passed the family which had so nobly cared for this stranger moved away, the grave became overgrown with wild weeds, and all that was left to mark the soldier's resting-place was the rough slab. This rotted by degrees, but was reverently replaced by some passer-by, and in this way the grave was kept marked; but it is doubtful if the few people who chanced to pass that way and see the slab ever gave a thought to the identity of the occupant of the grave, until after the election of Hon. James S. Hogg to the governorship of the State of Texas. Then someone of Chester County who had seen the grave wrote Governor Hogg concerning the dead soldier. In a short time a letter was received, stating that the soldier was Governor Hogg's father, and that he entered the Confederate army when the war first broke out, and had never been heard of by relatives or friends.

After more correspondence Governor Hogg caused the grave to be enclosed by a neat iron fence, and erected a handsome plain marble shaft over the grave. This monument bears the same simple inscription which marked the rough slab which had stood over the grave of one of the South's heroic dead.

Conceding the truth of the statement that General J. L. Hogg, of Rusk, Texas, died at a private house four miles west of Corinth, Miss., in the spring of 1862, was buried near by, and that his grave has been properly marked by his son, ex-Governor James S. Hogg, not a word of truth remains in the story, the remainder being fiction pure and simple, and the same may be refuted by a simple relation of the facts and circumstances of General Hogg's brief service in the Confederate army and his untimely death—facts that may easily be verified by the most creditable witnesses.

Joseph L. Hogg was appointed brigadier-general by the Confederate War Department in February, 1862. When his commission came he was ordered to report for duty at Memphis, Tenn., where he would be assigned to the command of a brigade of Texas troops. After the battle of Elkhorn a number of Texas regiments were ordered to cross the Mississippi River, among them the Third and Tenth Texas Cavalry— Company C of the Third and Company I of the Tenth were made up at Rusk. General Hogg's oldest son, Thomas E. Hogg, was a private in Company C, and these two regiments formed part of the brigade.

General Hogg met the Third Texas at Duvall's Bluff on

White River, where we dismounted, sent horses home, and went by steamer to Memphis, accompanied by General Hogg. (The battle of Shiloh was fought while we were on this trip.) After the delay incident to the formation of the brigade, getting up necessary supplies, etc., we were transported by rail, in command of General Hogg, to Corinth, or rather we were dumped off on the side of the railroad some two or three miles west of that town.   Here General Hogg remained in command of his brigade until he was taken sick and removed by the assistance of our very efficient surgeon, Dr. Wallace McDugald, attended by his negro body servant, Bob ————, than whom a more devoted, a more faithful and trustworthy slave never belonged to any man.

General Hogg was taken to a private house some two miles west of our camp, where he had every necessary attention until his death.   The faithful Bob was with him all the time. Dr. McDugald turned his other sick over to young Dr. Frazer, his assistant, and spent the most of his time with the General,— was with him when he died,—giving to him during his illness every medical care known to the science of his profession.

Thomas E. Hogg also was frequently with his father—was there when he passed away.   I visited General Hogg only once during his illness, some two or three days before his death. I was kept very busy during this time, and owing to a change in our camps I had to ride six or seven miles to see him, and only found one opportunity of doing so.   I found him as comfortably situated as could be expected for a soldier away from home, and receiving every necessary attention.

I will state that General Hogg came to us neatly dressed in citizen's clothes—never having had an opportunity of procuring his uniform, so that in fact he never wore the Confederate gray.   He was not wounded, was not under fire of the enemy; neither was his brigade, until the battle of Farmington, which occurred the day that General Hogg died.   After his death and after the army was reorganized, " for three years or during the war," Dr. McDugald,—who afterwards married General Hogg's daughter,—Dr. I. K. Frazer, Thomas J. Johnson, one of the General's staff, Thomas E. Hogg, and the ever-faithful Bob all came home, and of course related minutely to the widow, the two daughters, and the three minor boys, John

Lewis, and James Stephen, all the circumstances of the sickness, the lamented death and burial of the husband and father, Brigadier-General Joseph Louis Hogg.

Our camp was moved to a point about three miles east of Corinth. Decherd, the quartermaster, resigned and W. F. Rapley was appointed quartermaster by General Cabell. The rate at which our men fell sick was remarkable, as well as appalling, and distressing in the extreme. The water we had to drink was bad, very bad, and the rations none of the best. The former we procured by digging for it; the earth around Corinth being very light and porous, holding water like a sponge. When we first went there the ground was full of water, and by digging a hole two feet deep we could dip up plenty of a mean, milky-looking fluid; but as the season advanced the water sank, so we dug deeper, and continued to go down, until by the latter part of May our water holes were from eight to twelve feet deep, still affording the same miserable water. My horse would not drink a drop of the water the men had to use, and if I failed to ride him to a small running branch some two miles away he would go without drinking. The rations consisted mainly of flour, made into poor camp biscuit, and the most unpalatable pickled beef.

As fared General Hogg and his staff, so fared all the new troops who saw their first service at Corinth. While many of the old troops were taken sick, it was much worse with the new. We had one or two new Texas regiments come into our brigade, whose first morning report showed 1200 men able for duty;

two weeks from that day they could not muster more
than 200 men able to carry a musket to the front.
The sick men were shipped in carload lots down the
Mobile & Ohio Railroad, some dying on the trains,
and hundreds of others succumbing at the different
towns and stations where they were put off along
down that road south of Corinth. It seemed impossible for the surgeons and their assistants properly to care for the number of sick on their hands.
Day after day as I passed the Mobile & Ohio depot,
I saw scores of the poor sick fellows on the platform waiting to be hauled off. On the day we left
Corinth I passed Booneville, a station ten miles below
Corinth, and here were perhaps fifty sick men lying
in the shade of the trees and bushes. One of the attendants with whom I was acquainted told me he
had just returned from a tramp of two or three
miles, after water for a wounded man. At every
house he came to the well buckets had been taken
off and hid, and he finally had to fill his canteen with
brackish pond water. Why these sick men had been
put off here in the woods, when the station was the
only house in sight, where they could not even get
a drink of water, I do not know. The mere recollection of those scenes causes a shudder to this day.
I was told that two dead men were lying on the platform at Booneville, and a Federal scouting party
burned the station during the day. If it was true,
they were cremated.

As for myself, I was sick, but was on duty all the
time. I performed all the active duties of the
brigade quartermaster, being compelled to go to
Corinth and back from one to three times daily, look-

ing after forage and other supplies; carried all orders and instructions to the regimental quartermasters; superintended the moving of the trains whenever and wherever they had to be moved; and, in fact, almost lived in my saddle. But, with the exception of two or three nights spent with the troops at the front, when the day's duties were over, I was comfortably situated at headquarters, having a good wall tent, a cot, and camp-stool, and was kindly treated by General Cabell and the members of his staff. Dr. S. J. Lewis of Rusk was our brigade surgeon, and did everything he could for my comfort and, had I been well, my position would have been as pleasant as I could have desired in the army, as my duties mainly involved active horseback exercise, while my personal surroundings were very agreeable. Nevertheless, I lost my appetite so completely that I was unable to eat any of the rations that were issued to the army. I could no more eat one of our biscuits than I could have eaten a stone, and as for the beef, I could as easily have swallowed a piece of skunk. The mere sight of it was nauseating. Had I not been at headquarters doubtless I would have starved to death, since there we were able to get a ham or something else extra occasionally, and I managed to eat, but barely enough to keep soul and body together. Dr. Lewis saw me wasting away from day to day, and advised me to take a discharge —and quit the service; but this I declined to do. I paid General Hogg a short visit one afternoon during his illness, and another afternoon I rode over to Colonel Bedford Forrest's camp, to see my brother and some other Huntsville, Ala., friends. I found that my brother had gone, on sick leave, with Wallace Drake, one of his comrades, to some of Drake's relatives, down the railroad. With these exceptions I was not away from my post at any time. I must have gained some reputation for efficiency, as the quartermaster of our Arkansas regiment offered to give me half his salary if I would assist him in his office.

All the time we were at Corinth Major-General Halleck, with a large army, was moving forward from Pittsburgh Landing, on the Tennessee River, near the Shiloh battlefield, by regular approaches. That is, he would construct line after line of intrenchments, each successive line being a little nearer to us. Hence our troops were often turned out and marched rapidly to the front, in expectation of a pitched battle that was never fought, sometimes being out twenty-four hours. On one occasion an active movement was made to Farmington in an effort to cut off a division of the enemy that had ventured across Hatchie River, and the move was so nearly successful that the enemy, to escape, had to abandon all their camp equipage. On one of the days when our troops were rushing to the front in expectation of a battle, I came up with an old patriot marching along through the heat and dust under an umbrella, while a stout negro boy walking by his side carried his gun. This was the only man I saw during the war that carried an umbrella to fight under. As the battle failed to come off that day, I had no opportunity of learning how he would have manipulated the umbrella and gun in an engagement.

After General Hogg's death and the promotion of

Colonel Louis Hebert to brigadier-general, the Third Texas was transferred to Hebert's brigade, and I was temporarily separated from it. On May 8 our year's enlistment having expired, the men re-enlisted for three years, or during the war, and the regiment was reorganized by the election of regimental and company officers, when all the commissioned officers not promoted in some way returned to Texas. Captain Robert H. Cumby, of Henderson, was elected colonel, Captain H. P. Mabry, of Jefferson, lieutenant-colonel, and our Captain J. J. A. Barker, major. James A. Jones was elected captain of Company C, John Germany, first lieutenant, William H. Carr and R. L. Hood, second lieutenants. I was not present at the election. Dr. Dan Shaw, of Rusk County, was made surgeon of the regiment.

Finally, on May 28, we received orders to strike tents and have the trains ready to move. General Cabell came to my tent and advised me to go to the hospital, but I insisted that I could make it away from there on horseback. The next morning the trains were ordered out. Dr. Lewis, having procured about eight ounces of whisky for me, I mounted my horse and followed, resting frequently, and using the stimulant. About noon I bought a glass of buttermilk and a small piece of corn bread, for which I paid one dollar. This I enjoyed more than all the food I had tasted for several weeks.

On the day of the evacuation of Corinth, May 29, the Third Texas, being on outpost, was attacked by the enemy in force, and had quite a sharp battle with them in a dense thicket of black jack brush, but charged and gallantly repulsed them. Our new colonel and lieutenant-colonel not being able for service, Major Barker had asked our old Lieutenant-Colonel Lane to remain with us for the time, so the regiment was commanded by him and Major Barker. The regiment sustained considerable loss in this affair, in killed and wounded. Among the killed was my friend, the gallant young Major J. J. A. Barker ; our orderly sergeant, Wallace Caldwell, was mortally wounded, and John Lambert disabled, so that he was never fit for service again. For the gallant conduct of the regiment on this occasion, General Beauregard issued a special order complimenting the Third Texas, and specially designating a young man by the name of Smith, from Rusk County. Smith in the charge through the brush found himself with an empty gun confronting a Federal with loaded musket a few feet from him. The Federal threw his gun down on him and ordered him to surrender. Smith told him he would see him in Hades first, and turned to move off when the fellow fired, missed his body, but cut one of his arms off above the elbow, with a buck and ball cartridge. This was the kind of pluck that General Beauregard admired.* On that day the entire army was withdrawn and moved out from Corinth and vicinity. The manner and complete success of this movement of General Beauregard's has been very highly complimented by military critics.

* HEADQUARTERS WEST'N DEP'T.
BALDWIN. June 4, 1862.

General Order No. 62:

The General commanding takes great pleasure in calling the attention of the army to the brave, skillful and gallant con-

duct of Lieut. Col. Lane, of the Third Regt. Texas Dismounted
Cavalry, who with two hundred and forty-six men, on the 29th
ult., charged a largely superior force of the enemy, drove him
from his position, and forced him to leave a number of his
dead and wounded on the field.   The conduct of this brave regiment is worthy of all honor and imitation.   In this affair, Private J. N. Smith was particularly distinguished for brave and
gallant conduct in the discharge of his duty, and was severely
wounded.   To him, on some future occasion, will be awarded
a suitable " Badge of Honor."

By command of Gen'l Beauregard.

(Signed) : GEORGE W. BRENT, Acting Chief of Staff.

Private J. N. Smith, Third Texas Dismounted Cavalry.

Official copy.   M. M. Kimmell, Maj. & A. A. G.

CHAPTER VIl

BATTLE OF IUKA

IN the early days of June our command halted and
went into camp near Tupelo, Miss., where it remained
for several weeks. Here, as I was physically unfit
for service, I voluntarily abandoned my place at
General Cabell's headquarters and returned to my
own regiment. Obtaining, without difficulty, a
thirty days' furlough, I called on Dr. Shaw for
medicine, but he informed me that he had nothing
but opium, which would do me no good. But he
added, " You need a tonic; if you could only get
some whisky, that would soon set you up." Mounting my horse I went down into Pontotoc County,
and, finding a good-looking farmhouse away from
the public roads, I engaged board with Mr. Dunn,
the proprietor, for myself and horse for thirty days.
Mr. Dunn told me of a distillery away down somewhere below the town of Pontotoc, and finding a
convalescent in the neighborhood I sent him on my
horse to look for it, with the result that he brought
me back four canteens of " tonic."

Now Mr. Dunn's family consisted of that clever
elderly gentleman, his wife, and a handsome, intelli-
gent daughter, presumably about twenty years of

age. I soon realized that I had been very fortunate in the selection of a boarding house and that my lot for the next thirty days had been cast in a pleasant place, for every necessary attention was cheerfully shown me by each member of the family. They had lost a son and brother, who had wasted away with consumption, and in my dilapidated and emaciated condition they said I favored him, so they were constantly reminded of a loved one who had gone to his grave in about the same manner I seemed to be going, and they felt almost as if they were ministering to the wants of one of the family. They lived in a comfortable house, and everything I saw indicated a happy, well-to-do family. Their table, spread three times a day, was all that could be desired. We had corn bread, fresh milk and butter, fresh eggs, last year's yam potatoes, a plentiful supply of garden vegetables and other good things, everything brought on the table being well prepared. At first I had little or no appetite, but thanks to Miss Dunn's treatment, it soon began to improve. She, using the " tonic," gave me an egg-nog just before each meal, and, blackberries being plentiful, she gave me blackberries in every form, including pies and cordial, all of which, for one in my condition, was the best possible treatment.

So I improved and gained strength, not rapidly, but steadily, and though the thirty days was not as much time as I needed for a complete convalescence, it was all I had asked for. Mr. Dunn manifested a great deal of interest in my welfare; he did not think I could recover my health in the service, and urged me most earnestly to go back to camp, get a discharge, and go to Cooper's Well, a health resort down in Mississippi, and I was almost compelled to promise him I would do so, when in truth I had no such intention. The thirty days having expired, I bade farewell to these good people who had taken in a stranger and so kindly cared for him, and returned to camp, not strong or well by any means, but improved, especially in the matter of an appetite.

Going up to regimental headquarters upon my return to the command I let out my horse for his board, procured a rifle and at once reported to our company commander for duty. The strictest military discipline was maintained by General Louis Hebert in every particular, and one day's duty was very much like the duties of every other day, with a variation for Sunday. Of course the same men did not have the same duties to perform every day, as guard duty and fatigue duty were regulated by details made from the alphabetical rolls of the companies, but the same round of duties came every day in the week. At reveille we must promptly rise, dress, and hurry out into line for roll call; then breakfast. After breakfast guard-mounting for the ensuing twenty-four hours, these guards walking their posts day and night, two hours on and four hours off. Before noon there were two hours' drill for all men not on guard or some other special duty; then dinner. In the afternoon it was clean up camps, clean guns, dress parade at sundown; then supper, to bed at taps. On Sunday no drill, but, instead, we had to go out for a review, which was worse, as the men had to don all their armor, the officers button up their uniforms to the chin, buckle on their swords, and all march about two miles away through the dust and heat to an old field, march around a circle at least a mile in circumference, and back to camps. All that, including the halting and waiting, usually took up the time until about noon.

With the understanding and agreement that I would be excused from the drill ground when I broke down, and when on guard be allowed to rest when I had walked my post as long as I could, I went on duty as a well man. For quite a while I was compelled to leave the drill ground before the expiration of the two hours, and when I found I could not walk my post through the two hours some one of my comrades usually took my place. It was necessary for me to muster all my courage to do this kind of soldiering, but the exertion demanded of me and the exercise so improved my condition that soon I no longer had to be excused from any part of my duties. We had men in the command afflicted with chronic diarrhea who, yielding to the enervating influence of the disease, would lie down and die, and that was what I determined to avoid if I could.

Among other bugle calls we had " the sick call." Soon after breakfast every morning this, the most doleful of all the calls, was sounded, when the sick would march up and line themselves in front of the surgeon's tent for medical advice and treatment. Our surgeon, Dr. Dan Shaw, was a character worthy of being affectionately remembered by all the members of the Third Texas Cavalry. He was a fine physician, and I had fallen in love with him while he was a private soldier because he so generously exerted his best skill in assisting Dr. McDugald to save my life at Carthage, Mo. He was a plain, unassuming, jolly old fellow, brave, patriotic, and full of good impulses. He was the man who indignantly declined an appointment as surgeon soon after the battle of Oak Hills, preferring to remain a private in " Company B, Greer's Texas regiment," to being surgeon of an Arkansas regiment.

Knowing that he had no medicine except opium, I would go up some mornings, through curiosity, to hear his prescriptions for the various ailments that he had to encounter. He would walk out with an old jackknife in his hand, and conveniently located just behind him could be seen a lump of opium as big as a cannonball. Beginning at the head of the line he would say to the first one: " Well, sir, what is the matter with *you?* " " I don't know, doctor; I've got a pain in my back, a hurting in my stomach, or a misery in my head, or I had a chill last night." " Let me see your tongue. How's your bowels? " He would then turn around and vigorously attack the lump of opium with his knife, and roll out from two to four pills to the man, remarking to each of his waiting patients: " There, take one of these every two hours." Thus he would go, down the line to the end, and in it all there was little variation— none to speak of except in the answers of the individuals, the number of pills, or the manner of taking. And what else could he do? He had told me frankly that he had nothing in his tent that would do me any good, but these men had to have medicine.

For water at Tupelo we dug wells, each company a well, using a sweep to draw it. In this hilly por-

FRANK M. TAYLOR
First Captain of Company C, Third Texas Cavalry

tion of the State good water could be obtained by
digging from twenty to twenty-five feet.

From the time of the reorganization at Corinth
up to the middle of July Company C had lost a number of men. Some, as McDugald and Dillard, were
commissioned officers, and did not re-enlist; some were
discharged on applications, and others under the
conscription law then in force, a law exempting all
men under eighteen and over forty-five years of age.
Among those discharged I remember the two Ackers,
Croft, I. K. Frazer, Tom Hogg, Tom Johnson, W.
A. Newton, William Pennington, and R. G. Thompson, all of whom returned to Texas except William
Pennington, who remained with us a considerable
time, notwithstanding his discharge. In the regimental officers several changes had been made. After
the death of Major Barker, Captain Jiles S. Boggess, of Company B, from Henderson, was promoted
to major; Colonel R. H. Cumby resigned, and Lieutenant-Colonel Mabry was made colonel. J. S. Boggess, Lieutenant-Colonel, and Captain A. B. Stone,
of Company A, from Marshall, promoted to major.
About the first of August we moved up the railroad
to Saltillo, about fifteen miles north of Tupelo,
established camps, dug wells, and remained about
three weeks. Here the Fortieth (?) or Mississippi
regiment joined the brigade. This was a new regiment, just out from home, and it seemed to us, from
the amount of luggage they had, that they had
brought about all their household goods along. This
regiment is remembered for these distinct peculiar-
ities. Aside from the weight and bulk of its baggage
they had the tallest man and the largest boy in the

army, and the colonel used a camel to carry his private baggage. The tall man was rather slender, and looked to be seven feet high; the boy was sixteen or eighteen years old, and weighed more than three hundred pounds.

The brigade now consisted of the Third Texas, Whitfield's Texas Legion, the Third Louisiana, the Fourteenth and Seventeenth Arkansas, and the Fortieth Mississippi.* The army here, commanded by General Price, was composed of two divisions commanded by Generals Little and D. H. Maury. Many of the troops that came out of Corinth with General Beauregard had gone with General Bragg into Kentucky. At the end of three weeks we moved farther up the railroad to Baldwin. Here we dug more wells, and it was my fortune to be on the second day's detail that dug our company well. The first detail went down some eight feet, about as deep as they could throw the earth out. The next morning four of us, including C. C. Watkins and myself, the two weakest men, physically, in the company, were detailed to continue the digging. We arranged means for drawing the earth out, and began work, two at the time, one to dig and one to draw. At quitting time in the evening we had it down twenty-one feet, and had plenty of water. But we were not to remain long at Baldwin, as preparations for moving on Iuka were soon begun. As commissary supplies were gathered in for the approaching campaign they were stored in the freight department of the depot. One R. M. Tevis, of Galveston, was acting as commissary of subsistence, and

* Of this last I am not positive, but believe I am correct

Charlie Dunn, of Shreveport, was his assistant. They occupied a small room, the station agent's office, in the building during the day. A good many fatigue men were usually about the place during the day, to handle the stuff that was brought in.

One day, while I was on the platform, a country wagon drove up. Tevis and Dunn seemed to have expected its arrival, as they were soon out looking after the unloading. Among the rest was a barrel, a well-hooped, forty-gallon barrel, and instead of being sent in with the other stores it was hurriedly rolled into the private office of the commissary. This proved to be a barrel of peach brandy. Now, peach brandy was " contraband." The character and contents of the barrel were shrewdly guessed by the bystanders as it was hurried into its hiding-place, and its locality, after it had been stowed away, was clearly observed and mental note made thereof. The depot building was located at the north end of a cut and was elevated fully three feet above the ground, platforms and all. The Third Texas was camped along on the east side of the cut, say one hundred yards below the depot. The supplies were guarded day and night, the guards walking their beats, around on the platform. The next morning the guards were seen pacing the beats all right enough, but in the bottom of that barrel was an auger hole, and there was an auger hole through the depot floor, but there was not a gill of brandy in the barrel. At dress parade that morning it was unnecessary to call in an expert to determine that the brandy, when it leaked out, had come down the railroad cut. The two gentlemen most vitally interested in this occurrence dared not make complaint, but bore their sad bereavement in profound silence, and no one else ever mentioned it.

This brief stay at Baldwin terminated our summer vacation and our study of Hardie's infantry tactics. The constant all-summer drilling and the strict discipline we had been subjected to had rendered our dismounted cavalry the most efficient troops in the army, as they were good in either infantry or cavalry service, as was afterwards abundantly proved.

All things being ready, the march to Iuka was begun under General Price, with his two divisions. Up to this time the only infantry marching I had done, beyond drilling and reviews, was the two moves, Tupelo to Sattillo and Sattillo to Baldwin. As we were furnished transportation for cooking utensils only, the men had to carry all their worldly effects themselves and the knapsack must contain all clothing, combs, brushes, writing material and all else the soldier had or wished to carry, in addition to his gun, his cartridge box with forty rounds of ammunition, his cap box, haversack, and canteen. The weather was extremely hot, and the roads dry and fearfully dusty. While I had been on full duty for some time I was very lean, physically weak, and far from being well, and starting out to make a march of several days, loaded down as I was, I had some misgivings as to my ability to make it; but I did not hesitate to try. As the object of the expedition was to move on Iuka and capture the force there before General Grant could reinforce them from Corinth, a few miles west of that place, the troops were moved rapidly as practicable, the trains being left behind to follow on at their leisure. Unfortunately for me, I was on guard duty the last night before reaching our destination, and as we moved on soon after midnight I got no sleep.

Next morning after daylight, being within six or seven miles of Iuka, the Third Texas and Third Louisiana were placed in front, with orders to march at quick time into Iuka. Now, literally, this means thirty inches at a step and 116 steps per minute; practically it meant for us to get over that piece of road as rapidly as our tired legs could carry us. To keep up with this march was the supreme effort of the expedition on my part. I do not think I could have kept up if Lieutenant Germany had not relieved me of my gun for three or four miles of the distance. We found the town clear of troops, but had come so near surprising them that they had to abandon all their commissary stores, as they did not have time to either remove or destroy them. At the end of the march my strength was exhausted, and my vitality nearly so. The excitement being at an end, I collapsed, as it were, and as soon as we went into camp I fell down on the ground in the shade of a tree where I slept in a kind of stupor until nearly midnight.

We remained about a week in and around Iuka, in line of battle nearly all the time, expecting an attack by forces from Corinth; and as it was uncertain by which one of three roads they would come, we were hurried out on first one road and then another. One afternoon we were hurriedly moved out a mile or two on what proved to be a false alarm, and were allowed to return to camps. On returning we found a poor soldier lying in our company camp with a fearful hole in his head, where a buck and ball cartridge had gone through it. A musket was lying near him, and we could only suppose he was behind in starting on the march, and had killed himself accidentally.

On the night of September 18 we marched out about four miles on the Corinth road, leading west, and lay in line of battle until about 4 P. M. the next day, when a courier came in great haste, with the information that the enemy was advancing on the Bay Springs road from the south, with only a company of our cavalry in front of them. We had then to double quick back about three miles in order to get into the road they were on. We found them among the hills about one and a half miles from the town, a strong force of infantry, with nine or ten pieces of artillery, and occupying a strong position of their own selection. We formed on another hill in plain view of them, a little valley intervening between the two lines. Our fighting force consisted of General Little's division of two brigades, Hebert's, and a brigade of Alabama and Mississippi troops commanded by Colonel John D. Martin, and the Clark battery of four guns, Hebert's brigade in front of their center, with two of Martin's regiments on our right and two on our left. We began a skirmish fire, and kept it up until our battery was in position, when we began a rapid fire with canister shot. We then advanced in double line of battle, slowly at first, down the hill on which we had formed, across the little valley and began the ascent of the hill on which the enemy was posted, General W. S. Rosecrans in

command.   As we ascended the hill we came in range
of our own artillery, and the guns had to be silenced.
The entire Federal artillery fire was soon turned on
us, using grape and canister shot, and as their battery was directly in front of the Third Texas, their
grape shot and musketry fire soon began to play
havoc with our people, four of our men, the two files
just to my right, being killed.   We charged the battery, and with desperate fighting took nine pieces
and one caisson.   The horses hitched to the caisson
tried to run off, but we shot them down and took it,
the brave defenders standing nobly to their posts until they were nearly all shot down around their guns,
—one poor fellow being found lying near his gun,
with his ramrod grasped in both hands, as if he
were in the act of ramming down a cartridge when
he was killed.   The infantry fought stubbornly, but
after we captured their guns we drove them back
step by step, about six hundred yards, when darkness put an end to a battle that had lasted a little
more than two and a half hours, the lines being
within two hundred yards of each other.

I cannot give the number of Federal troops engaged in the battle, but General Rosecrans, in giving his casualties, enumerates eighteen regiments of
infantry, three of cavalry, one detached company,
and four batteries of artillery.   The cavalry was
not in the engagement, and I think he had but two
batteries engaged.   One of these, the Eleventh Ohio
Light Battery, lost its guns and fifty-four men.
The total Federal loss, reported, was 790, including
killed, wounded, and missing.   Hebert's brigade, that
did the main fighting, was composed of six regiments,

reporting 1774 for duty, and lost 63 killed, 305 wounded, and 40 missing; total, 408. Colonel Martin had four regiments (1405 men), and lost 22 killed and 95 wounded; total, 117. We had two batteries with us, the Clark battery and the St. Louis battery, but they only fired a few shots. The Third Texas had 388 men, and lost 22 killed and 74 wounded; total, 96. Company C lost W. P. Bowers, Carter Caldwell, W. P. Crawley, and W. T. Harris killed; and J. J. Felps severely wounded. Crawley had a belt of gold around his waist, but only four or five of us knew this, and I presume, of course, it was buried with him. General Maury's division was not engaged. General Henry Little, our division commander, was killed. Lieutenant Odell, of the Third Texas, who was acting regimental commissary, and who was mounted on my horse, was killed, and the horse was also killed. Colonels Mabry and Whitfield, and, I believe, all our other colonels were wounded. The captured artillery was drawn by hand into town that night, where the guns were left next morning, after being spiked, as we had no spare horses to pull them away. Spiking guns means that round steel files were driven hard into the touch-holes, giving the enemy the trouble of drilling these out before the guns can be of any use again.

As General Ord was marching rapidly with a strong force from Corinth to reinforce General Rosecrans, General Price concluded to retreat. Putting the trains in the road some time before daylight, early in the morning the troops marched out southward, leaving our wounded men in Iuka and sending a detail back to bury the dead. As General

Hebert's brigade had stood the brunt of the battle the evening before, we were put in front and, to clear the road for the other troops, we had to move at double quick time for six miles. This used me up, and I obtained permission to go as I pleased, which enabled me to outgo the command and to rest occasionally while they were coming up. We made a march of twenty-five miles that day on our way back to Baldwin. But oh, how my feet were blistered! They felt as if I had my shoes filled with hot embers. Late in the afternoon, when I was away ahead of the command I came to Bay Springs. This little village stands on a bluff of a wide, deep creek, and is crossed by a long, high bridge. At this time, when the creek was low, the bridge was at least twenty-five feet above the mud and water below. I climbed down under the bluff, just below the bridge, to a spring, where I slaked my thirst, bathed my burning feet and sat there resting and watching the wagons cross the bridge. Presently a six-mule team, pulling a wagon heavily loaded with ammunition in boxes, was driven onto the bridge, and as it was moving slowly along one of the hind wheels, the right one, ran so close to the edge that the end of the bridge flooring crumbled off and let the wheel down. Gradually this wheel kept sliding until the other hind wheel was off. This let the ammunition go to the bottom of the creek, followed by the wagon bed. Soon off came one fore wheel. This pulled off the other one, then the wagon tongue tripped the off-wheel mule and he dangled by the side of the bridge, and soon pulled the saddle mule off, and this process gradually went on, until the last mule started, and

as he fell off his hamestring caught on the end of
the bridge flooring, and for an instant the whole
outfit of wagon and six mules hung by the hamestring, when it broke and down went the wagon
and the six mules atop of it. The driver had seen
the danger in time to make his escape.

We soon arrived at Baldwin, our starting point.
Our wounded left at Iuka fell into the hands of the
enemy and were kindly treated and well cared for.
The good women of the town and surrounding country came to their rescue nobly, and they received
every necessary attention.

CHAPTER VIII

BATTLE OF CORINTH

Captain Dunn, the ."Mormon"—Paroles—Baldwin—On to Corinth—Conscription—Looking for Breakfast—The Army Trapped—A Skirmish—Escape—Holly Springs—Battle of Corinth—Casualties—Cavalry Again.

CAPTAIN DUNN, of Company F, was one of our badly wounded men, one of his legs having been broken by a grape shot. Captain Dunn was a unique character. He was a lawyer by profession, a very bright fellow, and lived at Athens, Tex. The first I ever knew of him he came to Rusk just before the war, to deliver an address to a Sunday-school convention. He was a very small man. In fact, so diminutive in stature that he was almost a dwarf. He was a brave, gallant soldier, a companionable, pleasant associate, and much of a wag. He was a great lover of fun, so much so that he would sacrifice comfort and convenience and risk his reputation in order to perpetrate a joke.

The ladies who came to nurse and care for our wounded soldiers at Iuka were like other women in one particular respect, at least,—they were desirous to know whether the soldiers were married or single, religious or otherwise, and if religious, their church relationship, denominational preferences and so on, and would converse with the boys with a view of learning these particulars. The usual questions were put to Captain Dunn by one of these self-sacrificing

111

attendants. He made no effort to deny that he was married and, with some hesitation, frankly acknowledged that he was a member of the church of the Latter Day Saints, usually called Mormons, which was enough information for one interview. With the exclamation, " Why, *you* a Mormon! " the woman retired. In whispers she soon imparted to all the other ladies who visited the hospital the astounding information that one of the Texas soldiers was a Mormon. They were incredulous, but after being vehemently assured by the interviewer that she had it from his own lips, some believed it was true, while others believed it was a joke or a mistake. To settle the question they appointed a committee of discreet ladies to ascertain the truth of the matter, and the committee promptly waited upon Captain Dunn. Without loss of time in preliminaries, the spokeswoman of the committee said: " Captain Dunn, we have heard that you are a Mormon and have come to you, as a committee, to learn the truth of the matter. Are you a Mormon? " " Yes, madam," said Captain Dunn. " Have you more than one wife? " " Yes," said Captain Dunn, " I have four wives." " Captain Dunn, don't you think it awful wrong? Don't you think it's monstrous to be a Mormon? " " No, madam," said Dunn, " that's my religion, the religion I was brought up in from childhood. All of my regiment are Mormons. All of them that are married have two or more wives. The colonel has six; some have four, and some five, just as they may feel able to take care of them." A meeting of the ladies was then called, an indignation meeting, and indignation was expressed in unmeas-

ured terms. The very idea! that they had scraped
lint, torn their best garments into bandages, had
cooked and brought soups and all the delicacies they
could prepare to the hospital—done all they could,
even to the offering up their prayers, for a detestable
Mormon, with four wives! It was unanimously resolved that it could be done no longer. From that
good hour, in passing through the hospital ministering to the wants of all the other wounded, they
gave Dunn not even as much as a look, to say nothing
of smiles, cups of cold water, soups, cakes, pies, and
other more substantial comforts.

This neglect of Captain Dunn was eventually noticed by the other soldiers, talked of, and regretted
by them and its cause inquired into. They earnestly
interceded with the ladies in his behalf, and urged
them that whatever Captain Dunn's faults might
be, he was a brave Confederate soldier, and had been
severely wounded in an attempt to defend their homes,
that he was suffering greatly from his wounds; that
if he was a Mormon he was a human being, and for
humanity's sake he deserved some attention and sympathy, and should not be allowed to die through neglect. This argument finally prevailed, the resolution
was rescinded, and the captain fared well for the
rest of the time, even better than he had before the
matter came up.

One day one of the ladies asked Captain Dunn
how it happened that he got his leg so badly crushed.
In the most serious manner he said to her: "Well,
madam, I am captain of a company, and when we
got into the battle the Yankees began shooting cannonballs at us, and to protect my men I got out in

front of them and would catch the cannonballs as they came and throw them back at the Yankees; but when the battle grew real hot they came so fast I couldn't catch all of them, and one of them broke my leg."

As soon as our men thought they were able to travel they were paroled and allowed to go free. When Captain Dunn was paroled he went to Texas for a rest, until he supposed he might be exchanged. On his return, he was traveling through Arkansas when a woman on the train asked him where he was going? He replied, "Madam, I am going to Richmond in the interest of the women of Texas. I am going to make an effort to induce the Confederate congress, in view of the great number of men that are being killed in the war, to pass a law providing that every man, after the war ends, shall have two wives."

When paroling our people their paroles were filled out by a Federal officer and presented to them for their signatures. The majority of the men cared little about the form, but only of the fact that they were to be allowed to go free until they were exchanged. But when they came to Colonel Mabry he read the parole over very carefully. He was described as H. P. Mabry, a colonel in the " so-called Confederate States Army." Mabry shook his head and said, " Sir, can you not leave out that ' so-called '? " He was informed that it could not be done. " Then," said the colonel, " I will not sign it." " In that case," said the officer, " you will have to go to prison." " Well," Mabry replied, " I will go to prison and stay there until I rot before I will sign a parole with that ' so-called Confederate States ' in it."

Captain Lee, of the Third Texas, was of the same way of thinking, and they both went to prison and remained there until they were exchanged, being sent to some prison in Illinois. Some months after they were exchanged and came back to us we captured some prisoners one day. One of them inquired if the Third Texas was there, and was told that it was. "Then," said he, "take me to Colonel Mabry or Captain Lee, and I'll be all right." This man was a " copperhead " whose acquaintance they had made while in prison. He didn't want to serve in the army against us, but had been drafted in, and was glad of an opportunity of changing his uniform.

At Baldwin about two days was spent in preparation for a march to Ripley, there to join General Van Dorn's command for a move on Corinth. I was on fatigue duty while at Baldwin, and had no time to recuperate after the hard campaign to Iuka and back, having been on guard duty the night before arriving at Ripley. We camped at that town one night and started next morning, September 29, 1862, for Corinth, General Van Dorn in command. On that morning I found myself with a fever, and feeling unequal to a regular march I obtained permission to march at will, and found Lieutenant R. L. Hood and F. M. Dodson in the same condition and having a like permit. We joined our forces and moved up the hot, dusty road about six miles. Being weary, foot-sore, and sick, we turned into the woods, lay down and went to sleep under some oak trees and did not wake until the beef cattle were passing us in

the afternoon. This meant that we had slept until
the entire army was ahead of us—cavalry, infantry,
artillery, and wagon train. We moved on until night
without overtaking our command. Nearing the village of Ruckersville it occurred to me that many
years ago this had been the post office of Peter Cotten, my mother's brother. Stopping at a house to
make inquiries, I learned that Willis Cook, his
son-in-law, lived only three-quarters of a mile west
of the village. We turned in that direction, and soon
found the place without difficulty. My call at the
gate was answered by my uncle at the front door.
I recognized his voice, although I had not heard it
since I was a small boy. Going into the house I made
myself known to him and his daughter, Mrs. Crook,
and received a cordial welcome, such a welcome as
made me and my comrades feel perfectly at home.
My good cousin, Tabitha, whose husband, Willis
Crook, was in the cavalry service, and in the army
then on its way to Corinth, soon had a splendid supper ready for us and in due time offered us a nice
bed. We begged out of occupying the beds, however, and with their permission stretched our weary
limbs under a shade tree in the yard and enjoyed a
good night's sleep.

Next morning one or two of the party had chills,
and we rested for the day. We soon learned that a
Federal cavalry command had dropped in behind our
army, and so we were cut off. Had we gone on in
the morning we would probably have been captured
during the day. Learning how we could find parallel
roads leading in the direction we wished to go, late
in the evening we started, traveled a few miles and

slept in the woods. The next morning we moved on until ten o'clock, and meeting a ten-year-old boy on a pony in a lane, we asked him if he knew where we could get something to eat. He said there was a potato patch right over there in the field. We asked him to whom it belonged, and he answered: "It belongs to my uncle; but he is laying out in the brush to keep out of the army;" and told us that his uncle lived up on the hill a short distance ahead of us. We did not go into the potato patch, but went up to the uncle's house. The house was a fairly good one, and in the front were two good-sized rooms with a wide, open hall. As we marched up to the rail fence in front of the house a woman came out into the hall, and we could see that the very looks of us aggravated and annoyed her. By way of getting acquainted with her, Dodson said: "Madam, have you got any water?" In a sharp, cracked voice, she answered: "I reckon I have. If I hain't, I would be in a mighty bad fix!" Having it understood that Dodson was to do the talking, we marched in and helped ourselves to a drink of water each, from a bucket setting on a shelf in the hall. During the next few minutes silence of the most profound sort prevailed. We stood there as if waiting to be invited to sit down and rest, but instead of inviting us to seats she stood scowling on us as if she was wishing us in Davy Jones' locker or some similar place. Hood and myself finally moved a little towards the front of the hall, and the following dialogue took place between Dodson and the woman: Dodson: "Madam, we are soldiers and are tired and hungry. We have been marching hard, and

last night we slept in the woods and haven't had anything to eat. Could we get a little something here? "
" No, you can't. I don't feed none of your sort.
You are just goin' about over the country eatin'
up what people's got, and a-doin' no good." " Why,
madam, we are fighting for the country." " Yes,
you are fightin' to keep the niggers from bein' freed,
and they've just as much right to be free as you
have." " Oh, no, madam ; the Bible says they shall
be slaves as long as they live." " The Bible don't say
no sech a thing." " Oh, yes, it does," said Dodson,
gently ; " let me have your Bible and I'll show it
to you." " I hain't got no Bible." " Madam, where
is your husband? " " That's none of your business,
sir ! " " Is he about the house, madam? " " No, he
ain't." " Is he in the army, madam? " " No, he
ain't. If you *must* know, he's gone off to keep from
bein' tuk to Ripley and sold for twenty-five dollars."
" Why, madam, is he a nigger? " " No, he ain't a
nigger ; he's just as white as you air, sir." " Well,
madam, I didn't know that they sold white men in
Mississippi." " No, you don't know what your own
people's a-doin'." During the conversation I kept
my eye on the lowest place in the fence. What she
said about being sold for twenty-five dollars was
in allusion to a reward of that amount offered by the
conscript authorities for able-bodied men who were
hiding in the brush to keep out of the army.

That night we lodged with a good old Confederate
who treated us the best he could. Next morning
Dodson bought a pony from him, which we used as
a pack-horse to carry our luggage. We then moved
much easier. Late in the evening we crossed Hatchie

River on the bridge over which the army had passed on its way to Corinth. Here we found Adam's Brigade and Whitfield's Legion guarding the bridge, that it might be used in the event of the army's being compelled to retreat. This bridge was only a short distance south of the Memphis & Charleston Railroad, and a few miles west of Corinth. We took the railroad and followed it nearly all night, turning off to sleep a little while before daylight. Early in the morning we struck across into the main-traveled road, and pushed on in an effort to rejoin our command. About nine or ten o'clock we came to a house, and determined to try for some breakfast, as we were quite hungry. We afterwards learned that a poor old couple occupied the house. Walking up to the front door we asked the old lady if we could get some breakfast, telling her we had been out all night and were hungry, and so on, the usual talk. She very readily said, yes, if we would wait until she could prepare it. She then invited us to come in and be seated, and said she would have the meal ready in a few minutes.

In a little while she came back and invited us in to breakfast in a little side room used for a kitchen and dining-room. As we started in I was in front, and as we entered the little dining-room and came in sight of the table she began to apologize because she was unable to give us anything more. I glanced at the table and saw a small, thin hoe-cake of corn bread and a few small slices of bacon, " only this and nothing more." I asked her if that was all she had. She answered that it was. Then I said, " Where are you going to get more when that is gone? " She

did not know.   Not doubting the truth of her statements, I said: " Madam, while we are hungry and
do not know when we will get anything to eat, we
could not take all you have.   While we are just as
thankful to you as if you had given us a bountiful
breakfast, we are soldiers, and can manage to get
something to eat somewhere, and will leave this for
you and your husband," and we bade her good-by
without sitting down to the table or tasting her
scanty offering.

This poor old woman, who must have been sixty
or more years old, had said, without a murmur and
without hesitation or excuse, that she would prepare
us some breakfast, and gone about it as cheerfully
as if she had had an abundance, cooking us all the
provisions she had, and only regretted she could not
do more for us,—this, too, when not knowing where
she would get any more for herself.

After leaving this humble abode we soon began to
meet troops, ambulances, and so on, and from them
we learned that our army was falling back.   Instead of going farther we stopped on the roadside
and waited for our command.   Noticing a squad of
soldiers out some distance from the road engaged
apparently about something unusual, my curiosity
led me out to where they were.   To my surprise I
found they were Madison County, Alabama, men,
most of whom I knew.   They were burying a poor
fellow by the name of Murry, whom I had known for
years, and who lived out near Maysville.   They
had rolled him up in his blanket and were letting
him down into a shallow grave when I approached,
and they told me that some of the boys that I knew

were wounded——in a wagon just across the road. I
soon found my old friends, John M. Hunter and
Peter Beasley, of Huntsville, Ala., in a common,
rough road-wagon. Poor Hunter! he was being
hauled over the long, rough road only that he might
die among his friends, which he did in a few days.
Beasley was not dangerously wounded.

We soon after joined our command .and marched
westward toward Hatchie bridge. But long before
we got there Generals Ord and Hurlbut had come
down from Bolivar, Tenn., with a heavy force of
fresh troops, had driven our guards away, and were
in undisputed possession of the crossing. Whitfield's Legion had been on the west side and had
been so closely crowded, with such a heavy fire concentrated on the bridge, that they had to take to
the water to make their escape.

Here was a problem confronting General Van
Dorn, a problem which must be speedily solved, otherwise a dire calamity awaited his whole army. These
two divisions of fresh troops were in front of an
army of tired, hungry, worn-out Confederates, with
General Grant's victorious army only a few miles in
our rear. What was called the boneyard road ran
some miles south of us and crossed the river on a
bridge at Crum's Mill; but this bridge, as a pre-
cautionary measure, had just been burned, and even
now its framework was still aflame. The route we
were on led west from Corinth parallel with, and but
a little south of, the Memphis & Charleston Railroad,
crossing Hatchie only a short distance south of Po-
cahontas. After crossing the river we would turn
south on the main Ripley road, and this road ran

parallel with the river, passing not far, three or four miles perhaps, west of Crum's Mill, so that a force might move rapidly from Corinth, on the boneyard road, cross at Crum's Mill and strike us in the flank and possibly capture our trains. Hence the precaution of burning this bridge. Everything of our army, whether on wheels, on foot, or on horseback, was now between Ord and Hurlbut in front and Grant and Rosecrans in the rear, without a crossing on Hatchie. The trains were parked, with a view, as I was told at the time, to burning them, leaving the troops to get out as they could, and we already had visions of swimming the stream. Personally I was wondering how much of my luggage I could get over with, and whether or not I could make it with a dry gun and cartridge box. General Price, in this dilemma, undertook to get the trains out, and he succeeded notably.

We had a pretty heavy skirmish with the forces at the bridge, with infantry and artillery, but only to divert attention from the trains as they moved out to gain the boneyard road. General Price went to the mill and, pulling down the gable end, cast it on the mill dam, and thus made a temporary bridge over which the trains and artillery were driven. Then that gallant old man, who had just proved himself to be as much at home acting as chief wagon master as when commanding his army corps, sat on his horse at the end of his unique bridge nearly all night, hurrying the wagons and artillery across. On the west bank of the stream he kept a bonfire alight, which threw a flickering glare across the bridge. As each teamster drove on to the east end of the

queer bridge he would slow up his team and peer
through the dim light for the proper and safe route.
Just as he would slow up one could hear the loud,
distinct voice of " Old Pap " shouting: " Drive up
there! Drive up! Drive up! Drive up!" And
thus it continued until every wheel had rolled across
to the west side of the Hatchie.

After we left the vicinity of the bridge and after
the skirmishing ceased, there was no time for order
in marching, unless it was with the rearguard; no
time to wait for the trains to stretch out into the
road and to follow it then in twos. We fell into the
road pell-mell, and moved in any style we wished to,
in among the wagons, or any way just so we moved
along and kept out of the way of those behind us.
During the afternoon, in the middle of the road, I
stumbled upon a small pile of corn meal, half a
gallon, maybe, that had sifted out of a commissary
wagon, and gathered part of it into my haversack,
mixed with a little dirt. I crossed the bridge away
along, I, suppose, about 11 P. M., after which I
stopped and watched General Price's maneuvers and
the crossing of the wagons until after midnight.

In the meantime I hunted around and found an
old castaway tin cup, dipped up some river water
and made up some dough, and then spreading it out
on a board, I laid it on General Price's fire until it
was partially cooked. Surely it was the most de-
licious piece of bread I have ever tasted, even to this
day.

When a good portion of the Third Texas had come
up we moved on into the Ripley road and were sent
northward for a mile or two, where we lay in line

of battle in ambush, near the road until the trains had all passed.

After daylight we moved on towards Ripley, being again permitted to march at will, as we had marched the night before. Approaching Ruckersville my heart turned again toward my good cousin, Tabitha Crook. Taking little David Allen with me, I made haste to find her home. Arriving there a short time before dinner, I said to her, " Cousin, I am powerful hungry." " Oh, yes," she said, " I know you are, Willis came by home last night, nearly starved to death." Soon we were invited into her dining-room and sat down to a dinner fit for a king. Here I met her brother, George Cotten, whom I had never seen before. After dinner Mrs. Crook insisted that we rest awhile, which we did, and presently she brought in our haversacks filled up, pressed down, and running over with the most palatable cooked rations, such as fine, light biscuits, baked sweet potatoes, and such things, and my mess rejoiced that night that I had good kins-people in that particular part of Mississippi, as our camp rations that night were beef without bread.

We then moved on to Holly Springs and rested for some days, after a fatiguing and disastrous campaign, which cost us the loss of many brave soldiers, and lost General Van Dorn his command, as he was superseded by General J. C. Pemberton.

The battle of Corinth was fought October 3 and 4, 1862. I do not know the number of troops engaged, but our loss was heavy. According to General Van Dorn our loss was: Killed, 594; wounded, 2162; missing, 2102. Total, 4858. The enemy reported: Killed, 355; wounded, 2841; missing, 319. Total, 3515. But if General Rosecrans stated the truth, our loss was much greater than General Van Dorn gave, as he (General R.) stated that they buried 1423 of our dead, which I think is erroneous. Company C lost our captain, James A. Jones, mortally wounded; John B. Long and L. F. Grisham, captured. As Captain Jones could not be carried off the field, Long remained with him and was taken prisoner, being allowed to remain with Captain Jones until he died. They were sent to Louisville, Ky., and then to Memphis, Tenn., where Captain Jones lingered for three months or more. After his death, Long, aided by some good women of Memphis, made his escape and returned to us.

It was at the battle of Corinth that the gallant William P. Rogers, colonel of the Second Texas Infantry, fell in such a manner, and under such circumstances, as to win the admiration of both friend and foe. Even General Rosecrans, in his official report, complimented him very highly. The Federals buried him with military honors. It was at Corinth, too, that Colonel L. S. Ross, with the aid of his superb regiment, the Sixth Texas Cavalry, won his brigadier-general's commission.

The evening before reaching Holly Springs we had what in Texas would be called a wet norther. Crawling in a gin-house I slept on the cotton seed, and when we reached Holly Springs I had flux, with which I suffered very severely for several days, as the surgeon had no medicine that would relieve me in the least. In a few days we moved south to Lumpkin's Mill, where we met our horses and were remounted, the Third, Sixth, Ninth and Whitfield's Legion composing the cavalry brigade, which organization was never changed. The army was soon falling back again, and continued to do so until it reached Grenada, on the south bank of Yalabusha River.

As we were now in the cavalry service we did the outpost duty for the army north of the Yalabusha.

JOHN GERMANY
Fourth and last Captain Company C, Third Texas Cavalry

FACING 126

CHAPTER IX

HOLLY SPRINGS RAID

At Grenada—Scouting—Engagement at Oakland—Chaplain Thompson's Adventure—Holly Springs Raid—Jake—The Bridge at Wolf River—I Am Wounded—Bolivar—Attack on Middleburg—Christmas.

WINTER weather came on us very early for the climate, snow having fallen to the depth of two or three inches before the middle of October, while the forests were still green, and the weather was intensely cold all during the fall months. While in this part of the field we had to be active and vigilant without having much fighting to do, and we enjoyed life fairly well.

General Washburn was sent out from Memphis with a force, estimated to be 10,000 men, and crossing Cold Water he came in our direction. The brigade in command of Lieutenant-Colonel John S. Griffith, of the Sixth Texas, moved up northwest to the little town of Oakland to meet him. Starting in the afternoon we marched through a cold rain which benumbed us so that many of us were unable to tie our horses when we stopped to camp at night. Next morning we passed through Oakland about ten o'clock and met the enemy a mile or two beyond and had a lively little engagement with them, lasting, perhaps, half an hour, in which our men captured a baby cannon, somewhat larger than a pocket derringer.

As we advanced in the morning, Major John H. Broocks, of the Legion, commanded the advance guard composed of a squadron of which our company was a part. About a half mile out of the little town, when we came to where the road forked, he halted and ordered me to take five men and go on the left-hand road a half or three-fourths of a mile, get a good position for observation, and remain there until he ordered me away. We went on and took our position, the main force moving on the right-hand road. Very soon they met the enemy and got into an engagement with them across a field nearly opposite our position. After awhile the firing having ceased, we heard our bugle sound the retreat, heard the brigade move out, and soon the Federals advanced until they had passed the forks of the road, when a battery began throwing shells at us. But no orders came from Major Broocks. Our position becoming untenable, and knowing we had been forgotten, and being unable to regain the road, we struck due south through the woods and rode all night, in order to rejoin the command. Finding it next morning, Major Broocks was profuse in his apologies for having forgotten us.

In the fight at Oakland we had about ten men wounded, Chaplain R. W. Thompson, of the Legion, voluntarily remaining to take care of them and dress their wounds. He had gotten them into a house and was very busy dressing the injury of one of them when a Federal soldier, with a musket in his hand, walked in and purposed making him a prisoner. Mr. Thompson was very indignant and stormed at the fellow in such a manner as to intimidate him, and he walked out and left him, and Thompson went on with his duties. Presently he was again accosted, and straightening himself up, he looked around to confront an officer and gaze into the muzzle of a cocked revolver. The officer asked, " Who are you? " " I am a Confederate soldier," said Thompson. " Then," said the officer, " I guess I'll take you up to General Washburn's quarters." " I guess you will not," replied Thompson. " Well, but I guess I will," said the officer. By this time Thompson was very indignant and said: " Sir, just take that pistol off me for half a minute and I'll show you whether I will go or not." " But," said the officer, " I am not going to do that, and to avoid trouble, I guess you had better come on with me." So Rev. Mr. Thompson went, and was soon introduced to the general, who said to him, " To what command do you belong, sir? " Thompson answered, " I belong to a Texas cavalry brigade." " Are you an officer or private? " inquired the general. " I am a chaplain," said Thompson. " You are a d——d rough chaplain," said the general. " Yes," replied the chaplain, " and you would say I was a d——d rough fighter if you were to meet me on a battlefield with a musket in my hands." " How many men have you in your command, sir? " asked the general, meaning the force he had just met. Mr. Thompson replied, " We have enough to fight, and we have enough to run, and we use our discretion as to which we do." The general stamped his foot in anger and repeated the question, and got the same answer. " You insolent fellow! " said the general, stamping his foot again. " Now," said Thompson in return, " let me say to you, General, that if you wish to gain any information in regard to our forces that will do you any good, you are interrogating the wrong man." " Take this insolent fellow out of my presence and place him under guard!" said the general. This order was obeyed, when a crowd soon began to gather around Thompson, growing larger and larger all the time and looking so vicious that Thompson was actually afraid they were going to mob him. Casting his eyes around he saw an officer, and, beckoning to him, the officer made his way through the crowd and soon dispersed it. Thompson's " insolence " cost him a long march—from there to the bank of the Mississippi River, where they released him, with blistered feet, to make his way back to his command.

Mr. Thompson was indiscreet, perhaps, in his manner, which was, no doubt, detrimental to himself; but he felt conscious that they had no right to detain him as a prisoner, or to interfere with his duties, and their manner irritated him. He was a good, whole-souled man, bold and fearless, and the best chaplain I knew in the army. What I could say about army chaplains, so far as my observation went, would not be flattering and, perhaps, had better be unsaid. But the Rev. R. W. Thompson, as chaplain of Whitfield's Texas Legion, was a success, and he was with us in adversity as well as in prosperity. When at leisure he preached to us and prayed for us; when in battle he was with the infirmary corps, bearing the wounded from the field, or assisting the surgeons in dressing their wounds and ministering to their wants. We all loved him, and thank God he was spared to do noble work for his Master and his church for many years after the Civil War was over, and I believe he is still living.

This Oakland affair occurred December 3, 1862. We had 1264 cavalry with a battery of four guns. Brigadier-General C. C. Washburn had 2500 men and two batteries. The engagement lasted about fifty minutes.

In the meantime General Grant had organized a fine army of about 75,000 men, including infantry, artillery, and cavalry, and was slowly moving down the Mississippi Central Railway. His front had reached as far south as Coffeeville, his objective point being Vicksburg, and he intended to co-operate with the river forces in taking that Confederate stronghold. General Pemberton's small army was gradually falling back before him. As the general depot of Federal supplies was at Holly Springs, and to destroy Grant's supplies might turn him back, or at least would cripple him more than the best fighting we could do in his front, this was determined on.

General Earl Van Dorn, who was known to be a fine cavalry officer, was just then without a command. Lieutenant-Colonel John S. Griffith, commanding a brigade, joined by the officers of the regiments composing the brigade, about the 5th of December petitioned General Pemberton to organize a cavalry raid, to be commanded by General Van Dorn, for the purpose of penetrating General Grant's rear, with the idea of making an effort to destroy the supplies at Holly Springs, and to do any other possible injury to the enemy. In due time the raid was or-

ganized.   We took Holly Springs, captured the
guards, destroyed the supplies, and General Grant
was compelled to abandon his campaign.

From this time General Van Dorn commanded us
until his untimely death at the hands of an assassin.
A more gallant soldier than Earl Van Dorn was not
to be found, and as a cavalry commander I do not
believe he had a superior in either army.   What I
may say about this, however, here or elsewhere, I
know is of little worth, as most people have formed
and expressed an opinion——some in favor of Forrest,
some Stuart, and some Joe Wheeler ; but any man
who was with us on this expedition and at other
times, and who watched General Van Dorn's maneuvers closely, studied his stratagems and noted the
complete success of all his movements, would have
to admit that he was a master of the art of war in
this line of the service.   At the head of an infantry
column he moved too rapidly, too many of his over-
marched men failed to get into his battles ; but place
him in front of good men well mounted, and he
stood at the head of the class of fine cavalry commanders.

With three brigades, ours, General W. H. Jackson's and Colonel McCulloch's, aggregating about
3500 men in light marching order, without artillery,
we moved from the vicinity of Grenada early after
dark, about the 18th of December, and marched rapidly all night.   We passed through Pontotoc next
day, when the good ladies stood on the street with
dishes and baskets filled with all manner of good
things to eat, which we grabbed in our hands as we
passed rapidly through the town.   After passing

Pontotoc a command of Federal cavalry dropped in on our rear, fired a few shots and picked up some of our men who had dropped behind. Among those picked up was our Indiana man, Harvey N. Milligan. Somehow the boys had come to doubt Milligan's loyalty, and suspected that he had fallen behind purposely to allow himself to be captured. When the rear was fired on the colonel commanding the rear regiment sent a courier up to notify General Van Dorn. The fellow came up the column in a brisk gallop. Now, to pass from the rear to the front of a column of 3500 cavalry rapidly marching by twos is quite a feat, but he finally reached General Van Dorn, and with a military salute he said: "General, Colonel ——— sent me to inform you that the Yankees have fired on his rear!" "Are they in the rear?" inquired the general. "Yes, sir," answered the courier. "Well, you go back," said the general, "and tell Colonel ——— that that is exactly where I want them." It was interesting to note how adroitly he managed to keep in our rear on the entire expedition all their forces that attempted in any way to interfere with our movements. Their scouts were, of course, watching us to determine, if possible, our destination.

In going north from Pontotoc, General Van Dorn, instead of taking the Holly Springs road, passing east of that place, headed his command towards Bolivar, Tenn. Their conclusion then was, of course, that we were aiming to attack Bolivar. Stopping long enough at night to feed, we mounted our horses and by a quiet movement were placed on roads leading into Holly Springs, dividing the command into two columns, so as to strike the town by two roads. We moved slowly and very quietly during the night, and while we were moving directly towards the town guards were placed at the houses we passed lest some citizen might be treacherous enough to inform the enemy of our movements. The road our column was on was a rough, unworked, and little used one. At the first appearance of dawn, being perhaps three miles from town, we struck a gallop and, meeting no opposition, we were soon pouring into the infantry camps near the railroad depot, situated in the eastern suburbs. The infantry came running out of the tents in their night clothes, holding up their hands and surrendered without firing a gun. Our other column encountered the mounted cavalry pickets, and had a little fight with them, but they soon galloped out of town, and on this bright, frosty morning of December 20, A. D. 1862, the town, with its immense stores of army supplies, was ours. Standing on the track near the depot was a long train of box cars loaded with rations and clothing only waiting for steam enough to pull out for the front. This was burned as it stood. Leaving the Legion to guard the prisoners until they could be paroled, the Third Texas galloped on uptown. The people, as soon as it was known that we were Confederates, were wild with joy. Women came running out of their houses, to their front gates as we passed, in their night robes, their long hair streaming behind and fluttering in the frosty morning air, shouting and clapping their hands, forgetting everything except the fact that the Confederates were in Holly Springs! On every hand could be heard shouts—

" Hurrah for Jeff Davis! Hurrah for Van Dorn! Hurrah for the Confederacy!"

A mere glance at the stores—heaps upon heaps of clothing, blankets, provisions, arms, ammunition, medicines, and hospital supplies for the winter, all for the use and comfort of a vast army—was overwhelming to us. We had never seen anything like it before. The depot, the depot buildings, the machine shops, the roundhouse, and every available space that could be used was packed full, and scores of the largest houses uptown were in use for the same purpose, while a great number of bales of cotton were piled up around the court-house yard. One large brick livery stable on the public square was packed full, as high as they could be stacked, with new, unopened cases of carbines and Colt's army sixshooters, and a large brick house near by was packed full of artillery ammunition.

For about ten hours, say from 6 A. M. to 4 P. M., we labored destroying, burning, this property, and in order to do this effectually we had to burn a good many houses. Riding out in the afternoon, to the yard where the wagons were being cut down and burned, I found numbers of mules and horses running at large, some of our men turning their lean horses loose and taking big fat captured horses instead. Just then it occurred to me that I had no horse of my own in Mississippi, my mount having been killed at Iuka. John B. Long being in prison when the horses came, I was using his. Now, if I only had some way of taking one of these horses out. Starting back uptown, puzzling over this problem, I met a negro boy coming out of a side street, and

hailed him.   In answer to my inquiries he said his
name was Jake, and belonged to Mr. ——— down
at Toby Tubby's ferry on the Tallahatchie.   "What
are you doing here?" I inquired.   "Dese Yankees
has bin had me prisoner."   After a little further
colloquy he readily agreed to go with me.   "Cause,"
said he, "you-all done whipped de Yankees now. Dey
bin braggin' all de time how dey could whip de rebels
so fast, and when you all come in here dis mornin'
dey went runnin' everywhere, looking back to see if
de rebels was comin'.   I done see how it is now.   I
don't want nothin' more to do with dese Yankees.
I'se bin hid under de floor all day."   I took one of
the abandoned horses, procured a mule for Jake to
ride, with saddle, bridle and halter, and taking the
outfit uptown said to Jake: "Now, when we start
you fall in with the other negroes, in the rear, and
keep right up, and when we camp you inquire for
Company C, Third Texas Cavalry—and hold on to
the horse at all hazards."   I had no further trouble
with Jake.   He carried my instructions out all right.
About 4 P. M., having finished our day's work, we
moved out of the northeast part of the town, and
looking back we saw the Federal cavalry coming in
from the southwest.

In this raid we captured about 1500 prisoners, according to General Van Dorn, and General Grant
said the same.   They were commanded by Colonel R.
C. Murphy of the Eighth Wisconsin Infantry.   Poor
Murphy! he was peremptorily dismissed from the
service without even a court martial. General Grant
estimated their loss in supplies destroyed at $400,-
000, while General Van Dorn's estimate was $1,500,-

000. Doubtless one was too low and the other one
too high. We marched out a few miles and camped
for the night, and all the evening we could hear the
artillery cartridges exploding in the burning buildings.

The next day early we were on the march northward. That morning when I awoke I felt a presentiment that if we had to fight during that day I
would be wounded, and no effort of mine was sufficient to remove the impression, even for a moment.
As the weather was quite cold, visions of the horrors
of going to prison in midwinter troubled me, since
a wound that would put me past riding my horse
would mean that I would be left to fall into the
enemy's hands. Near noon we came to Davis' Mill,
near the Tennessee line, not far from Lagrange,
Tenn., where we made an effort to destroy a railroad
bridge and trestle on Wolfe River. It was guarded
by 250 troops, commanded by Colonel William H.
Morgan of the Twenty-fifth Indiana Infantry. We
were fooling about this place three hours perhaps,
and it was late before I understood the meaning
of our maneuvers. Our brigade was dismounted,
double-quicked here and double-quicked there, double-
quicked back to our horses, remounted, galloped off
to another place, double-quicked again somewhere
else and back to our horses. Then, remounting, we
took another gallop and double-quicked again to the
only tangible thing I saw during the day, and that
was to charge a blockhouse or stockade.

The enemy was in what they called a blockhouse,
constructed by taking an old sawmill as a foundation
and piling up cotton bales and cross-ties, and throw-

ing up some earthworks. Approaching this by a
wagon road we came to a bridge across a slough perhaps two hundred yards from their fort. We met
their first bullets here, as part of their fire could be
concentrated on this bridge. Crossing a little river
bottom, entirely open except for a few large white
oak trees, we came to a bridge across Wolfe River
about seventy yards from their works. To charge
in column across this bridge under their concentrated
fire was the only chance to get to them, but coming
to this bridge we found that the floor was all gone,
leaving only three stringers about ten inches square,
more or less, on which we could cross. Running
along the bank up the river to the right was a levee
some three feet high. The men in front, five or six
impetuous fellows, running on to the stringers, one
of them fell as he started across, and the others
crossed the river. When I reached the bridge the
command was deploying behind the levee without attempting to cross. I remained near the bridge. By
this time I was more fatigued, I thought, than I had
ever been, with the perspiration streaming off my
face, cold as the day was. Here we kept up a fire
at the smoke of the enemy's guns, as we could not
see anything else, until a courier could find General
Van Dorn, inform him of the situation and ascertain his wishes as to the advisability of our attempting to cross the river. Anxious to know what had
become of the men that went onto the bridge, I rose
up and looked over the levee. One of them had been
killed and was lying in the edge of the water, and
the others were crouched under the opposite bank of
the river out of immediate danger. While this ob-

servation only required a moment of time and a moment's exposure above the levee, I distinctly felt a minie ball fan my right cheek. While I had not doubted for a moment that I was going to be shot somewhere sometime during the day, this narrow escape of having a minie ball plow through my cheek was very unpleasant. The thought of the ugly scar such a wound would leave flashed into my mind, and wondering where I was to be wounded I settled down behind the levee and continued firing my Sharps' rifle without exposing myself. Finally we were ordered to fall back. As soon as we were on our feet, and while crossing the little bottom, we would again be exposed to the enemy's fire, so the command fell back at double-quick. I rose and started, and, looking around, I saw Lieutenant Germany fall, and turned back to assist him, supposing he was shot; but as I approached him he jumped up and passed me, laughing, having merely stumbled and fallen. This threw me behind everybody. I soon found I was so fatigued that I could not double-quick at all, so I slowed up into an ordinary walk. The command, in the meantime, to avoid the fire that could be concentrated on the slough bridge, had flanked off to the left some distance above, and crossed on chunks and logs that had fallen in the slough. Very soon I was the only target for the men in the blockhouse, and they shot at me for sheer amusement. At last a ball struck me on the right thigh. Thinking it was broken, I stopped, bearing all my weight on my left foot, and, selecting a large white oak near by, intending, if I could not walk to manage somehow to pull myself behind this to shield myself, I waited for " something to turn up." Soon learning, however, that my thigh was not broken, I moved on. Rather than lose time in going up to where the command had crossed and run the risk of being left behind, supposing that on reaching the horses they would mount and move off, I determined to cross on the bridge, which I did in a slow walk, and am sure there was no less than a hundred shots fired at me. Somehow I felt that I was not going to be shot more than once that day, so even after I got across the bridge and lay down to drink out of a little pool of water in the road, their bullets spattered water in my face. I managed to get off with the command, and while my wound was slight it bled freely and caused me a good deal of pain, as I had to ride constantly for several days, and was unable to dismount to fight any more on this trip.

We camped not far from Davis' Mill, and crossed the Memphis & Charleston Railroad early next morning, cutting the telegraph wires, tearing up the track, burning cross-ties, and bending and twisting the rails. Leaving, we struck a gallop towards Sommerville, Tenn., and galloped nearly all day. Entering Sommerville unexpectedly, we created a little consternation. There was a Union mass meeting in the town, and, there being no thought that there was a Confederate soldier in a hundred miles of them, they were having an enthusiastic time. Some of the old gentlemen, pretty boozy on good Union whisky, stood on the streets and gazed at us with open mouths. I heard one old fellow yell out, " Hurrah for Sommerville! " Another one standing near him yelled out, " Oh, d———n Sommerville to h———l ; I say hurrah for the soldiers!" The good ladies, however, when they learned who we were, began bringing whatever they had to eat, handing it to us as we passed along. Camping a few miles out, next morning we took the road leading to Jackson, Tenn., a road which passes west of Bolivar. In the afternoon, however, we changed our course, traveling by roads leading eastward, and camped several miles north of Bolivar.

Next morning, December 24, by making demonstrations against Bolivar, General Van Dorn induced the enemy to gather all his forces in the vicinity for its defense, including 1500 cavalry under Colonel Grierson, sent by General Grant in pursuit of us. We moved down a main road leading into Bolivar from the north, formed fours, driving in their cavalry scouts and infantry pickets to the very suburbs of the town, where the column was turned to the right through alleys, byways, and vacant lots until we were south of the town, when moving quietly out southward, we thus again had all our opposition in our rear. Moving down the railroad seven miles, Middleburg was attacked. As our troops dismounted and formed a line, Ed. Lewis, of Company B, was killed. I remained mounted, with the horses. The command moved up into the town and found the enemy in a brick house with portholes, through which they fired. This was not taken. Of Company C, A. A. Box was killed here. After staying for two hours, perhaps, we moved off just as the enemy's cavalry from Bolivar came up and fired on our rear.

The next point threatened was Corinth, in order

to concentrate the forces in that neighborhood. Leaving Middleburg, we passed through Purdy, took the Corinth road, and moved briskly until night, went into camp, fed, and slept until 1 A. M., when we saddled up, mended up the camp-fires and moved through neighborhood roads, into the Ripley road. Reaching Ripley at noon we rested, fed, and ate our Christmas dinner. In about two hours we moved out, and looking back we could see the enemy's cavalry from Corinth entering the town. They fired a piece of artillery at us, but as they were in our rear we paid no attention to them. Crossing the Talla-hatchie at Rocky Ford we camped on the banks of the stream. Here General Van Dorn waited for the enemy until noon the next day, but Colonel Grierson, who was pretending to follow us, never put in an appearance. In the afternoon we moved to Pontotoc and camped there that night in a terrible drenching rain. We then moved leisurely back into our lines, with " no one to molest us or make us afraid."

CHAPTER X

THE ENGAGEMENT AT THOMPSON'S STATION

January, 1863—Jake Arrested—Detailed—My Brother Visits Me—Elected Second Lieutenant—Battle of Thompson's Station—Duck River—Capture of the Legion—The " Sick Camp "—Murder of General Van Dorn.

" THE Holly Springs raid," never to be forgotten by the participants therein, having now become a matter of history, we rested for a time. January, 1863, came, and with it a great deal of rain, making mud very abundant and the roads very bad. During one of these cold rainy days, who should come pulling through the mud nearly half a leg deep, but the " aforesaid Harvey N. Milligan, late of Indiana." He had made his escape from the enemy, and, minus his horse, had made his way back to us through the rain and mud afoot. " I told you Milligan was all right," was a remark now frequently to be heard. A day or two after this, word came around that there were a half dozen horses at regimental headquarters to be drawn for by the companies. I went up to represent Company C, and drawing first choice, I selected a horse and gave him to Milligan. During that same year he deserted on that very horse, and rode him into the Federal lines.

My boy Jake having brought my horse out of the enemy's lines, of course I expected he would wish to return home, and I proposed to give him the mule and let him go to his master. But no, he begged me to allow him to stay with me, to feed and attend to my horse, do my mess duties and such work. Of course I could not drive him off. This boy, eighteen or nineteen years old, perhaps, became a splendid servant, and as much devoted to me, apparently, as if I had raised him. Some months after this we were passing through Columbus, Miss., one day, and his owner, happening to be there, saw him, arrested him and sent him home. When I heard of it that night of course I supposed I would never see Jake any more, but to my surprise he came back in a short time, mounted on a splendid mule. When I started back to Texas in February, 1865, Jake was anxious to go with me, but I gave him a horse and saddle, and told him to take care of himself.

The severe horseback service we had had since the battle of Corinth, and our diet, principally sweet potatoes, had restored my health completely, my wound had healed, and I was in good condition to do cavalry service. At this time, too, I was detailed to work in the regimental quartermaster's department. We were ordered to middle Tennessee, and started through the cold mud. My present position put me with the trains on a march, and we had a great time pulling through the mud, and in some places we found it almost impassable. Crossing the Tennessee River a short distance below the foot of Mussell Shoals we struck the turnpike at Pulaski, Tenn., proceeding thence to Columbia, and then, crossing Duck River a few miles below that place, we moved up and took position near Springhill in front of Franklin, and about thirteen miles south of that place.

One evening soon after we went into camp on the turnpike some ten miles below Columbia, two men rode into the camp inquiring for me. I soon learned that it was my brother, accompanied by "Pony" Pillow, who had come for me to go with them to Colonel Billy Pillow's, who lived on a turnpike three or four miles west from the one we were on. Obtaining permission, I then accompanied them. My brother had been sick for some time, and had been cared for by the Pillows, first by Granville Pillow's family and then by Colonel Billy's family. He had now recovered and was about ready to return to his command, which was on the right wing of General Bragg's army, while we were camped on the extreme left.

I found Colonel Billy Pillow to be a man of ninety-four years, remarkably stout and robust for a man of his age. His family consisted of a widowed daughter, Mrs. Smith, who had a son in the army; his son, "Pony" Pillow; and his wife. This old gentleman was a cousin to my grandmother Cotten, and had moved with her family and his from North Carolina when they were all young people. They told me of my grandmother's brother, Abner Johnson, who had lived in this neighborhood a great many years, and died at the age of 104 years. The next day we visited Colonel Pillow's sister, Mrs. Dew, a bright, brisk little body, aged ninety-two years, and the day following we spent the day at Granville Pillow's. Granville Pillow was a brother of General Gideon J. Pillow, and nephew of Colonel Billy. He was not at home, but we were welcomed and well entertained by Mrs. Pillow and her charming young married daughter, whose husband was in the army. Mrs. Pillow inquired to what command I belonged, and when I told her I belonged to a Texas command, she asked me if I was an officer or private? When I told her I was a private, she said it was a remarkable fact that she had never been able to find an officer from Texas, and that the most genteel, polite and well-bred soldier she had met during the war was a Texas private. She added that while Forrest's command had camped on her premises for several weeks, and many of them had come into her yard and into her house, she never had found a private soldier among them. This was in keeping with the " taffy " that was continually given the Texas soldiers as long as we were in Tennessee.

In the afternoon, bidding my brother farewell, I left him, overtaking my command, as it had finished crossing Duck River and was camped on the north bank.

Franklin is situated on the south bank of Big Harpeth River, being fortified on the hills north of the river overlooking the town. General Van Dorn established his headquarters at Spring Hill, about thirteen miles south of Franklin, on the Franklin and Columbia turnpike. Brigadier-General W. H. Jackson was assigned to duty as commander of a division composed of Whitfield's Texas brigade and Frank C. Armstrong's brigade. Many of the Texas boys were very indignant, at first, that General Jackson, a Tennessean, should be placed over them—so much so that they hanged him in effigy. He was sensible enough to pay no attention to this, but went on treating us so kindly and considerately that we all learned to respect him and like him very much.

Some time in the early part of this year, 1863, Colonels J. W. Whitfield and Frank C. Armstrong were appointed brigadier-generals. Near the end of February, I think, John B. Long returned to us, and reported the death of our captain, James A. Jones, having remained with him until he died in Memphis, after which J. B. made his escape. First Lieutenant John Germany now being promoted to captain, and Second Lieutenant W. H. Carr promoted to first lieutenant, this left a vacancy in the officers, which was filled by my election by the company as second lieutenant. So I gave up my position with the quartermaster and returned to the company, quitting the most pleasant place I had ever had in the army, for Captain E. P. Hill, our quartermaster, was one of the best and most agreeable of men, my duties were light, and my messmates and associates at headquarters good, jolly fellows.

Our duties in front of Franklin were quite active, as we had several important roads leading southward to guard, and frequent skirmishes occurred, as the pickets usually stood in sight of each other on the hills that were crossed by the turnpike roads, especially on the main Columbian pike. In addition to the Columbia pike, running directly south from Franklin, there was Carter's Creek pike, leading southwest, and the Lewisburg pike, leading southeast. Still no considerable fighting was done until the 4th day of March, which culminated in the battle of Thompson Station on the 5th. On the 4th, Colonel John Coburn of the Thirty-third Indiana Volunteers was ordered out by General Gilbert, with a force of nearly 3000 men, including infantry, cavalry, and about six pieces of artillery, to proceed to Spring Hill and ascertain what was there.   About four miles from Franklin they were met by a portion of General Van Dorn's command, and pretty heavy skirmishing resulted, when both armies fell back and camped for the night.   Our forces retired to Thompson's Station, nine miles south of Franklin, and went into camp south of a range of hills running across the pike just south of the station.   This is a very hilly country, and the Nashville & Decatur Railroad runs through a little valley between two ranges of hills, and the station is in the valley a short distance west of Columbia pike.

On the morning of the 5th the enemy was found to be advancing again, and leaving our horses behind the hill, we crossed over to the north side, and near a church just south of the station we were formed behind a stone fence—that is, Whitfield's brigade, other troops to our right and left, our artillery being posted to our right on the hill near the pike.   The enemy advanced to the range of hills north of the station, on which was a cedar brake.   From our position back to the hill and cedar brake was an open field with an upgrade about half a mile wide, the station, with its few small buildings, standing in between the lines, but much nearer to us.   The Federal artillery was posted, part on each side of the pike, directly in front of ours, and the batteries soon began playing on each other.   Colonel Coburn, not seeing our line of dismounted men behind the stone fence, ordered two of his infantry regiments to charge and take our batteries, and they came sweeping across the field for that purpose. When they came to within a short distance of our front, Whitfield's brigade leaped over the fence, and, joined by the Third Arkansas, of Armstrong's brigade, charged them, and soon drove them back across the open field, back to the hill and cedar brake, their starting point. Here they rallied, and being re-enforced they drove our forces back to the station and stone fence, where, taking advantage of the houses and stone fence, our forces rallied and, being joined by the remainder of General Armstrong's brigade, drove them back again. This attack and repulse occurred three successive times. In the meantime General Forrest, with two regiments of his brigade, had been ordered to move around to the right and gain their rear, and as they retired to their hill and cedar brake the third time, Forrest opened fire on their rear, and they threw down their guns and surrendered—that is, those that were still upon the field. Their artillery, cavalry, and one regiment of infantry had already left.

The engagement lasted about five hours, say from 10 A. M. to 3 P. M. Our loss was 56 killed, 289 wounded, and 12 missing; total, 357. The enemy's loss was 48 killed, 247 wounded, and 1151 captured; total, 1446. Among the captured were seventy-five officers, including Colonel Coburn, the commander, and Major W. R. Shafter, of the Nineteenth Michigan, who is now Major-General, and one of the heroes of the Spanish-American war.*

* Since the above was written Major-General William Rufus Shafter had been placed upon the retired list. In the fall of 1906 he was stricken with pneumonia, near Bakersfield, Cal., where he died November 12, after a short illness.

Company C lost Beecher Donald, mortally wounded. Among the killed of the Third Texas of my acquaintances I remember Drew Polk (alias "Redland Bully"), of Company E, and Sergeant Moses Wyndham, a friend of mine, of Company A. From the day of the Oak Hill battle up to this day we had never been able to get T. Wiley Roberts into even a skirmish, but to-day he was kept close in hand and carried into the battle, but ran his ramrod through his right hand and went to the rear as related in this chronicle. Among the losses was Colonel S. G. Earle, of the Third Arkansas, killed; and my friend H. C. Cleaver, an officer in the same regiment, was wounded. Rev. B. T. Crouch of Mississippi, a chaplain, was killed while acting as aide-de-camp to General Jackson. Captain Broocks, brother of Lieutenant-Colonel John H. Broocks, was also killed.

The dwelling houses in the vicinity of Thompson's Station were situated in the surrounding hills overlooking the battlefield, but out of danger, and from these houses a number of ladies witnessed the battle. When they saw the enemy being driven back they would clap their hands and shout, but when our forces were being driven back they would hide their eyes and cry. Thus they were alternately shouting and crying all day, until they saw nearly twelve hundred of the enemy marched out and lined up as prisoners, and then they were permanently happy.

Here we lost the beautiful flag presented to us in the Indian Territory, the staff being shot in two, while in close proximity to the enemy. The bearer picked it up, but as he had to make his escape through

JESSE W. WYNNE
Captain Company B, Third Texas Cavalry

a plum thicket the flag was torn into narrow ribbons and left hanging on the bushes.

General Van Dorn had four brigades under his command at this time—Forrest's brigade of four regiments and a battalion, Martin's brigade of two regiments, Armstrong's brigade of two regiments, one battalion, and one squadron, and Whitfield's brigade of four Texas regiments. All these participated, more or less, in the battle, but as Jackson's division was in the center the brunt of the battle fell on them, as the losses will show. Whitfield lost 170 men, Armstrong, 115, Forrest, 69, and Martin, 3.

General Gordon Granger took command at Franklin immediately after the battle of Thompson Station. He and General Van Dorn were said to be classmates at West Point, and good friends personally, but it seemed that they made strenuous efforts to overreach or to out-general each other.

About March 8 another expedition was sent out by the enemy apparently for the purpose of driving us out of the neighborhood. Skirmishing began on the Columbia and Lewisburg pikes, some three or four miles south of Franklin, and was continued on the Columbia road for about three days, until we fell back across Rutherford Creek and took a strong position behind a range of hills south of the creek, destroying the bridges. In the meantime heavy rains were falling, the creek rising so that General Granger's forces were delayed about two days in their efforts to cross, and all that could be done was to skirmish across the creek. Duck River, just behind us, rose so high and ran so swift, that pontoon bridges could not be maintained across it. A battle could not be risked with only a small ferryboat in such a stream. Still the skirmishing went on, until the trains and artillery were ferried across, when, leaving skirmishers on the hill to deceive the enemy, we moved up the river through cedar brakes to White's bridge, twenty miles, crossed to the south side of the river, and when the enemy crossed Rutherford Creek they found no rebels in their front. We moved down through Columbia, and five or six miles down the Mount Pleasant turnpike and went into camp.

" Pony " Pillow's wife had been kind enough to knit me a pair of fine yarn gauntlets, and having heard that we had crossed Duck River, she sent them to me, by her husband, who came up soon after we struck camp. While he was there I was ordered to take a squad of men whose horses needed shoes, go into the country and press one or two blacksmith shops, and run them for the purpose of having a lot of shoeing done. I got my men and went home with Pillow, took charge of shops in the neighborhood, and was kept on duty there about eight days, staying with my old grand-cousin's family every night. I enjoyed this opportunity of talking with the old gentleman very much, as he had known my maternal grandparents when they were all children in Guilford County, North Carolina, before the Revolutionary War. He, himself, had been a soldier for eight years of his life, and had been shot through the body with a musket ball. In these war times he loved to talk about his exploits as a soldier. While I was there he mounted his horse and rode several miles through the neighborhood, to the tanyard and the shoe shop, to

procure leather and have a pair of boots made for his
grandson, who was in the army.

The work of shoeing the horses having been completed, and Duck River having subsided, we crossed
back to the north side again, taking up our old position near Spring Hill, and resumed our picketing
and skirmishing with General Granger's forces.   It
is unnecessary, even if it were possible, to allude to
all these skirmishes.   The picket post on Carter's
Creek pike, eight miles from Franklin, was regarded
as important for some reason, and an entire regiment
from our brigade was kept there.   One regiment for
one week and then another regiment for the next,
and were sent there with strict orders to have horses
saddled and everything in readiness for action at daybreak in the morning.   The Third Texas had been
on the post for a week, and was relieved by the Legion
under Lieutenant-Colonel Broocks.   The Legion had
been there two or three days, and had grown a little
careless, as nothing unusual had ever happened to
any of the other regiments while on duty there.   Just
at daybreak one morning in the latter part of April
Granger's cavalry came charging in upon them and
completely surprised them in their camps, before they
were even up, and captured men, horses, mules,
wagons, cooking utensils—everything.   Colonel
Broocks and some of his men made their escape,
some on foot and some on horseback, but more than
a hundred were captured, their wagons cut down and
burned, their cooking utensils broken up, and their
camp completely devastated.   One of the escaped men
came at full speed to our camps, some three miles
away, and as quick as possible we were in our saddles

and galloping towards the scene of the disaster—
but we were too late. We galloped for miles over
the hills in an effort to overtake the enemy and re-
capture our friends, but failed.

We all felt a keen sympathy for Colonel Broocks
and his men, for no officer in the army would have
felt more mortification at such an occurrence than
the brave, gallant John H. Broocks. It was said
that he was so haunted by the sounds and scenes of
the capture of his regiment that he was almost like
one demented, and that for days and days afterwards he would sit away off alone on some log, with
his head down, muttering, " Halt! you d——d rebel,
halt! "

At one time during April General Van Dorn, with
a goodly number of his command, made a demonstration upon Franklin, drove in all their outposts, and,
selecting the Twenty-eighth Mississippi Cavalry and
leading it himself, he charged into the heart of the
town.

The night following the race we made after the
Broocks' captors, my horse fell sick and became unfit
for service. In consequence I was ordered to send
him to the pasture in charge of the command, a few
miles below Columbia, and take command of " the
sick, lame, and lazy camp " on Rutherford Creek, a
temporary camp made up of slightly disabled men,
and men with disabled horses or without horses. I
was on duty here two weeks, with about as little to
do as could be imagined. It was while I was on duty
here that General Van Dorn's death occurred at his
headquarters at Spring Hill. He was assassinated
by one Dr. Peters, who was actuated by an insane

jealousy. Dr. Peters was an elderly man, with a pretty young wife; General Van Dorn was a gay, dashing cavalier. Dr. Peters was in the general's office when he came in from breakfast, and asked the general to sign a pass permitting him to pass through the picket lines. As General Van Dorn was writing his signature to the paper, Dr. Peters stood behind him. When Van Dorn had given the last stroke with the pen, the doctor shot him in the back of the head, and, having his horse ready saddled, he mounted and galloped up to our pickets, passed through, and made his escape. As soon as the crime was known a number of the general's escort mounted their horses and gave chase, but they were too late to stop the doctor.

In a few days after this very sad occurrence General Jackson's division was ordered to Mississippi by rapid marches, and about the middle of May we reluctantly bade adieu to this beautiful, picturesque middle Tennessee.

CHAPTER XI

THE SURRENDER OF VICKSBURG

Moving Southward—I Lose My Horse—Meet Old Huntsville Friends—A New Horse—In Mississippi—" Sneeze Weed " —Messenger's Ferry—Surrender of Vicksburg—Army Retires —Fighting at Jackson—After Sherman's Men—A Sick Horse —Black Prince—" Tax in Kind "—Ross' Brigade—Two Desertions.

I now disbanded my important command on Rutherford Creek, and telling my men that every fellow must take care of himself, I joined the movement towards Mississippi. Leaving in the afternoon, we camped on the north bank of Duck River opposite Columbia. That night while walking into a deep gully I sprained an ankle very badly. Next morning my foot and ankle were so swollen I could not wear my boot, so I exchanged it for an old rusty brogan shoe found in an ambulance, and shipped all my luggage in the ambulance. I made my way to the pasture eight miles below, mounted my horse and joined the command.

Before reaching camp that night my horse was taken with a peculiar lameness in one of his hind legs. Next morning soon after starting he became lame again, and grew rapidly worse, so much so that I fell behind, being unable to keep up. Soon I had to dismount and lead him, driving him and urging him along in every possible way, spending the day in that manner, and walking most of the time. In the after-

noon I saw that contingent called stragglers.   One
man rode up and said to me, " Hello, Barron! you
are gone up for a horse.   You'll have to have another.   Have you got any money? "   " Not much,"
I replied.   Pulling out a one hundred dollar bill, he
said : " Here, take this ; it will do you some good."
During the afternoon another, and after a while still
another passed me, saying and doing precisely the
same thing.   Crossing Elk River just before dark,
I stopped to spend the night at the first house on
the road.   The next morning my horse was dead.   I
had expected to trade him, but now I was completely
afoot, encumbered with my rigging, fifteen miles behind the command, which had gone on the Athens,
Ala., road.

After visiting the lot I went back to breakfast,
feeling that I was a good many miles from home, but
not particularly daunted.   I had all the time believed
that a soldier who volunteered in the Confederate
army in good faith and was honestly doing his duty
would come out of all kinds of difficulties in good
shape.   After breakfast I watched the road until
noon.   At last a man of our brigade came along
leading a horse, and I inquired to whom he belonged.
" One of the boys that was sent to the hospital."   I
then explained to him my situation.   " All right,"
said he, " you take this pony, find you a horse, and
leave the pony with the wagon train when you come
to it."   " The pony " was a shabby little long-haired
mustang with one hip bone knocked down, but I was
mounted for the time.

It was now Saturday afternoon.   I was only thirty
miles from Huntsville and might find a horse there,

so it occurred to me, but I had no desire to go there
at this time.   In the condition circumstances had
placed me, I only wished to procure a horse suitable
for my necessities and follow my command.   I
mounted the mustang and took the Huntsville road,
inquiring for horses along the way.   I stayed all
night at Madison Cross roads, and was not recognized by the man at whose house I spent the night,
although I had been acquainted with him for several
years.   I went out next morning, Sunday as it was,
and examined and priced one or two horses in the
neighborhood, but found I could not pay for one
even if I had fancied him, which I did not.   So I
continued my course towards Huntsville, jogging
along very slowly on my borrowed horse, as the
weather was quite warm.   When within two or three
miles of town I left the Pulaski road and turned in
through some byways to the residence of Mr. Tate
Lowry, a friend of mine who lived near the Meridian-
ville pike, a mile or two out of town.   I rode up to
his place about noon, just as he had returned from
church.   He extended me a very cordial welcome to
his house, which was only occupied by himself, his
good old mother, and little boy.   We soon had a
good dinner.   Out in the office I enjoyed a short
sleep, a bath, and began dressing myself, Mr. Lowry
coming in and placing his entire wardrobe at my
service.   I was soon inside of a nice white shirt and
had a pair of brand new low-quartered calfskin shoes
on my feet.   He then brought me a black broadcloth
frock coat, but there I drew the line.   Having a neat
gray flannel overshirt, I donned that, buckled on my
belt and felt somewhat genteel.   As there were to be

religious services at the Cumberland church in the afternoon, we agreed to go into town. We walked in, however, as I had no disposition to show the mustang to my friends in town, and when we arrived at the church we found the congregation assembled and services in progress. I went quietly in and seated myself well back in the church, and when the services ended everybody, male and female, came up to shake hands, all glad to see me, among them my home folks, Mrs. Powers ("Aunt Tullie"), and Miss Aggie Scott, her niece. I accompanied them home, and met Mr. W. H. Powers, with whom I had lived and worked for several years, and who was my best friend. I found it a delightful experience to be here after an absence of more than three and half years. Of course I explained to them why I was in Huntsville and how I became lame. On Monday morning Mr. Powers called me in the parlor alone, and said to me, "Do you need any money?" "That depends," I said, "on the amount a horse is going to cost me." "Well," he said, "if you need any, let me know, and at any time that you need any money, and can communicate with me, you can get all the Confederate money you need." During the day our L. H. Reed came in from the command, bringing me a leave of absence to answer my purpose while away from the command.

Here I met my friend (Rev. Lieutenant-Colonel W. D. Chadick), who said to me upon learning my purpose in this neighborhood: "I have a good horse I bought very cheap, to give my old horse time to recover from a wound. He is about well now, and as I cannot keep two horses you can have him for what

he cost me." "How much was that?" "Three
hundred dollars." "All right," said I, "the three
one hundred dollar bills are yours, and the horse is
mine." This animal was a splendid sorrel, rather above
medium size, about seven years old, sound as a dollar,
and a horse of a good gaits.   When I had gone forty
miles from Huntsville one thousand dollars of the
same currency would not have bought him.   On
Tuesday I had him well shod, mounting him the next
morning, and while I was sorely tempted to remain
longer, I started for Mississippi.   I really had a
very bad ankle, and could have called on an army surgeon and procured an extension of my leave and
spent a few days more in this delightful way, but
hoping to be well enough to perform the duties that
came to my lot by the time I reached the command,
I pulled myself away.

I went out and got the pony, left the borrowed
articles of clothing, and crossing Tennessee River at
Brown's Ferry, I laid in corn enough before I left
the valley to carry me across the mountains where
forage was scarce.   I strapped it on the pony and
made good time to Columbus, Miss.   Here I was
detained several hours by Captain Rice, the post commander, much against my will.   He claimed that he
was ordered by General Jackson, in case he found
an officer in the rear of the command, to detain him
until he gathered up a lot of stragglers, who were
to be placed in charge of the officer, to be brought
up to the command.   After worrying me several
hours, he turned me over a squad of men, and I
started out with them.   As soon as I crossed the
Tombigbee River I turned them all loose, and told

them I hoped they would go to their commands; as for me, I was going to mine, and I was not going to allow a squad of men to detain me for an instant.

I passed through Canton about dark one evening, and learning what road the command was probably on, having left my pony as per instructions, I rode into our camp just at midnight. The next morning we moved to Mechanicsburg, loaded, capped, and formed fours, expecting to meet the enemy, which, however, did not prove to be the case. I therefore was able to be at my post by the time the first prospect of a fight occurred.

On my way down one day, I passed where the command had camped on a small creek, and noticing several dead mules I inquired into the cause, and was told they were killed from eating " Sneeze weed," a poisonous plant that grows in middle and southern Mississippi. I learned to identify it, and as we had several horses killed by it afterwards, I was very careful when we camped, to pull up every sprig of it within reach of my horse.

On the long march from Spring Hill, Tenn., to Canton, Miss., Company C had the misfortune to lose four men—Dunn, Putnum, and Scott deserted, and McCain was mysteriously missing, and never heard of by us again.

General U. S. Grant had swung round with a large army through Jackson, Miss., fought a battle with General Pemberton at Raymond and another at Baker's Creek, Champion Hill, where General Pemberton was driven back, having General Loring's division and twenty pieces of his artillery cut off.

Pemberton was compelled to fall back across Big Black River at Edward's Depot into Vicksburg with the remainder of his army, and General Grant had thrown his army completely around Vicksburg on the land side, and that city was besieged.   We were sent down here to hover around the besieging army, to see that they " 'have deyselves, and keep off our grass."   The large gunboats in the river, above and below, with their heavy ordnance were bombarding the city.   These huge guns could be heard for many miles away, from early morning until night.   When I first heard them I inquired the distance to Vicksburg, and was told it was a hundred miles.   During the siege we had active service, driving in foraging parties, picketing, scouting, and occasionally skirmishing with the enemy.

About the first of July we drove the enemy's pickets from Messenger's Ferry, on Big Black River, and held that crossing until the 5th.   Vicksburg was surrendered on the 4th, and on the evening of the 5th our pickets were driven from the ferry by a large force under General Sherman, who began crossing the river and moving east.   General Joseph E. Johnston was in command of our army outside of Vicksburg, and at the time the city was surrendered he was down on Big Black, with his forces and a train loaded with pontoons—everything indicating his intention to attempt a cut through the enemy's line to relieve General Pemberton.   As soon as the surrender occurred General Johnston began falling back towards Jackson, and we fought the advancing enemy several days while he was making this retrogressive movement.   We fought them daily, from early in the morning until late in the afternoon, holding them in check, though some days they advanced several miles and others only two or three, owing to the nature of the ground and the more or less favorable position afforded us. This detention gave General Johnston time to move his trains and infantry back at leisure and to get his army in position in front of Jackson. Finally falling back to Jackson, we passed through our infantry lines in front of the city and took our position on the extreme right wing of our army, beyond the northern suburbs of the city. Jackson, it may be well to state, is located on the west bank of Pearl River. General Sherman's right wing rested on Pearl River south of the city, and his lines extended in a semicircle around the west of the city. Here we fought more or less for about a week, with some pretty severe engagements, directly in front of the city. In passing through the northern portion of the city to the position assigned to us we passed the State Lunatic Asylum. After we formed a line and everything was quiet, there being no enemy in our front, Joe Guthery, of Company B, sauntered out and reconnoitered a little and upon his return he approached Captain Jesse Wynne and said: "Captain, you ought to see General Johnston's fortifications down by the asylum. He's got a great big swiege gun planted there that demands the whole country around."

One afternoon our works were assaulted by a brigade of General Lauman's division, who were almost annihilated. For this move he was promptly superseded, as it was claimed he acted without orders. After some heavy fighting in front of the city I chanced to pass our field hospital where the surgeons were at work, and just behind the hospital I looked into an old barrel about the size of a potato barrel and discovered it was nearly full of stumps of arms and legs, bloody and maimed, just as they had fallen under the knife and saw. This to me was so ghastly a sight that I never remember it without a shudder.

As we had heretofore been dismounting to fight, I had not had an opportunity of trying my new horse under fire until now. We had a long line of skirmishers in extension of our line to the right in front of us and three or four hundred yards from a line of the enemy's skirmishers. They were in the brush not exposed to view, so a desultory fire was kept up all along the line. I was sent up the line to deliver some orders to our men, and as I had to ride up the entire line and back, the enemy's skirmishers soon began firing at me, and kept it up until I made the round trip, the minie balls constantly clipping the bushes very near me and my horse. This completely demoralized him, and he would jump as high and as far as he possibly could every time he heard them. Some horses seem to love a battle, while others are almost unmanageable under fire. The first horse I rode in the army was lazy and had to be spurred along ordinarily, but when we were going into a battle and the firing began he would champ the bits, pull on the bridle, and want to move up.

After some four days in front we were sent to the rear of Sherman's army, where we captured a few wagons and ambulances and destroyed some cotton, and upon returning encountered the enemy's cavalry at Canton. While we were on this enterprise General Johnston had retired from Jackson and fallen back to Brandon, and General Sherman, after a few days, returned to Vicksburg. Our brigade now moved out into Rankin County for a rest. Here orders were issued for thirty-day furloughs to one officer and three men of the company. As Lieutenant Hood was away on sick leave, I proposed to Lieutenant Carr that we would concede Captain Germany the first leave. No, he would not do that; he was as much entitled to it as Captain Germany. "All right," said I; "then we'll draw for it, and I will be sure to get it." The drawing turned out as I had prophesied, and I presented the furlough to Captain Germany. The furloughs those days had a clause, written in red ink, "provided he shall not enter the enemy's lines," and that meant that in our case our men should not go to Texas.

In this "Siege of Jackson," as General Sherman called it (July 10-16, 1863), the enemy's reported losses in killed, wounded and missing numbered 1122. I am unable to give our losses, but in the assaults they made we lost very few men. General Sherman had three army corps on this expedition.

Our rest near Pelahatchie Depot was of short duration, as we were soon ordered back to guard the country near Vicksburg on the Big Black and Yazoo Rivers, with headquarters at Bolton Station. During Sherman's occupation of Jackson he had destroyed miles of railroad track, bridges, and depots, and had also destroyed rolling stock, including passenger cars, flat cars, and locomotives. Now in August a force of their cavalry came out from Memphis and undertook to steal all the rolling stock on the Mississippi Central Railroad. They came down about as far as Vaughan's Station and gathered up the rolling stock, including a number of first-class locomotives, intending to run them into Memphis or Grand Junction. We were sent after them and had a lively race. As they were about twenty-four hours ahead of us they would have succeeded, doubtless, had not some one burned a bridge across a small creek opposite Kosciusko. As may be imagined, we gave them no time to repair the bridge. We moved about a hundred miles in two days, with no feed for men or horses except green corn from the fields.

Reaching Durant very late at night in a drenching rain we were turned loose to hunt shelter in the dark as best we could, and we had a great time getting into vacant houses, under sheds, awnings, in stables or any available place that we might save our ammunition. At Old Shongolo, near Vaiden, the good ladies had prepared a splendid picnic dinner for us, but as we could not stop to partake of it they lined up on each side of the column as we passed, with waiters loaded with chicken, ham, biscuit, cake, pies, and other tempting viands and the men helped themselves as they passed, without halting.

One evening we stopped just before night to feed, for the horses were hot and tired, and our men hungry and in need of sleep. The horses were hastily attended to, that we might get some sleep, as we were to remain here until midnight, then resume the march. At starting time I found my horse foundered. Groping my way through the darkness to General Whitfield's headquarters, I told him I could not go on, for my horse was foundered.   " Old Bob's in the same fix," he said.   " Cross Big Black River as soon as you can, and go back to the wagon train, and tell that fellow that has got old Bob to take good care of him."

As the command moved off I started in the opposite direction.   I had only gone a short distance when I came up with Lieutenant Barkley of the Legion, in the same sad condition.   After daylight we stopped to breakfast at a house on the road, then crossed the Big Black, and, as our horses grew worse, we made a short day's travel and spent the night with Mr. Fullylove, a generous old gentleman.   Next morning the horses traveled still worse.   About 10 A. M. we came to the residence of Hon. Mr. Blunt, of Attalah County, and decided that, with the permission of the family, we would remain here until morning.   Consulting Mrs. Blunt, she said: " Mr. Blunt is not at home.   The only persons with me are my daughter and a young lady visiting us; but if I knew you were gentlemen I would not turn you off."   We told her we were Texans, and claimed to be gentlemen—and we remained there until the next morning.   After caring for our horses we were invited into the parlor or sitting-room and introduced to the young ladies.   The visitor was Miss Hattie Savage, who lived only a few miles away.   Soon the usual interrogatory was propounded.   " Are you gentlemen married? "   Barclay answered: " Yes, I am married.   I have a wife and baby at home," and exhibited the little one's picture.   I told them I was not so fortunate as to be married.   Soon we had a good dinner and spent quite a pleasant day.   The next morning, with many thanks for the generous hospitality we had enjoyed, we said good-by to the three ladies.

I found that my horse's condition grew constantly worse, so that now he could scarcely get along at all. After traveling about three miles we came to the house of Mr. Leftwich Ayres, who proved to be a very excellent man. Seeing the condition of our horses, he invited us to remain with him until morning, which we did. At this time and ever afterward I received only kind and generous treatment from all the members of this family, which consisted of Mr. Ayres, his wife and her grown daughter, Miss Joe Andrews. A Mr. Richburg owned and operated a tanyard and boot shop near the Ayres place. I visited his shop and left my measure for a pair of boots, and found Mr. Richburg to be a most excellent man. He made me several pairs of boots afterwards. Next morning Mr. Ayres said to me: " Your horse cannot travel. Old Arkansaw is the only horse I have; take him and ride him, and I will take care of your horse until he is well." I accepted the proposition, and Barclay and myself returned to our commands.

General Whitfield followed the Federals to Duck Hill, near Grenada, without overtaking them, and returned to Canton, and to Big Black and Yazoo Rivers.

When I supposed from the lapse of time that my horse had recovered, I obtained permission and went after him. Reaching Mr. Ayres' home about ten o'clock one morning, he met me at the gate and told me that my horse was about well, that he had just turned him out for the first time to graze. I immediately felt uneasy, and being anxious to see him we walked around his inclosure and soon found him; but as soon as I came near him I saw the effects of the deadly sneeze weed, and in spite of all we could do for him in a few hours he was dead. Mr. Ayres was very much grieved and said, " I would not have had your horse die at my house under the circumstances for a thousand dollars. There's old Arkansaw; take him and make the best you can of him— ride him, trade him off, or anything." I therefore returned to the command on Old Arkansaw, a pretty good old one-eyed horse.

It is not possible now to remember all the movements made by us during the next two or three months, the number of foraging parties we drove back or the number of skirmishes with the enemy. As I have said I returned to the command mounted on Old Arkansaw, but did not keep him long, as I traded him for a pony, and traded the pony for a mule, a splendid young mule, good under the saddle, but not the kind of a mount I desired. Awaiting for a favorable time, I obtained leave to go to Huntsville, where I could obtain money to buy another horse. I soon made the distance over the long road at the rate of forty miles per day on my mule. Passing through Tuscaloosa one morning, after a travel of thirty-two miles, I put up with Mr. Moses McMath, father-in-law of General Joseph L. Hogg. Here I found General L. P. Walker, our first Secretary of War, who had started to Huntsville. We traveled together as far as Blountsville, he relating to me many interesting facts about the early days of the Confederate army, and here we learned that a division of Federal cavalry was then in Madison County.

At Warrenton, in Marshall County, I met Hop Beard, son of Arthur Beard, who had lost one of his hands in Forrest's cavalry, and had a horse which he was now willing to sell. From Warrenton I went to Lewis' Ferry on Tennessee River, fifteen miles below Huntsville. Here I found my half-brother, J. J. Ashworth. Crossing the river at this place I went up on the Triana road as far as William Matkin's, about seven miles from Huntsville. Here I found Miss Aggie Scott, of the household of my friend, W. H. Powers, and was advised that it was unsafe to go to town. I therefore sent a message to Mr. Powers by Dr. Leftwich, who lived in the neighborhood, and he brought me seven hundred dollars. With this I returned to Warrenton and purchased a splendid black horse of Mr. Beard, really the best horse for the service that I had owned. I called him Black Prince. With the horse and mule I returned to Mississippi. I had met several Huntsville people at Warrenton, among them my friend Tate Lowry. He insisted that when I got back to Noxubee County, Mississippi, that I stop and rest at his plantation. I reached there about ten o'clock one rainy day, and remained there until next morning. I found his overseer a clever, agreeable man, and the plantation a very valuable property, and was shown the fine stock and everything of interest on the place. Noticing a long row of very high rail pens filled with corn, I remarked on the fine crop of corn he had made. " Oh," said he, " that is only the tax in kind where I throw every tenth load for the Government."

And that was really only one-tenth of his crop! Our government claimed one-tenth of all produce, which was called "tax in kind."

As I passed through Macon I was offered five hundred dollars for my mule, but I had determined to carry it back and give it to Mr. Ayres in place of Old Arkansaw. I rode up to Mr. Ayres' house about three o'clock in the afternoon, presented him with the mule, and remained there until morning. While there Mrs. Ayres gave me enough of the prettiest gray jeans I ever saw, spun and woven by her own hands, to make a suit of clothes. I sent to Mobile and paid eighty-five dollars for trimming, such as buttons, gold lace, etc., and had a tailor make me a uniform of which I justly felt proud.

In September, perhaps it was, General Whitfield, on account of failing health, was transferred to the trans-Mississippi department, and the Rev. R. W. Thompson, the Legion's brave chaplain, also left us and recrossed the Mississippi. The brigade was commanded alternately by Colonel H. P. Mabry, of the Third Texas, and Colonel D. W. Jones, of the Ninth, until Colonel L. S. Ross, of the Sixth Texas, was appointed brigadier-general and took permanent command of us, and the brigade was ever after known as Ross' Brigade. Colonel Mabry was given command of a Mississippi brigade and sent down on the river below Vicksburg.

Early in December we attempted to capture a foraging party that came out from Vicksburg. Starting early in the night, Colonel Jones was sent with the Ninth Texas around to intercept them by coming into the road they were on near the outside breastworks. The command moved slowly until morning, when coming near the enemy we gave chase, galloping ten miles close at their heels. When they passed the point Colonel Jones was trying to reach he was in sight. We ran them through the outer breastworks and heard their drums beat the long roll. When we turned about to retire two of our men, Milligan and Roberts, fell back and entered the enemy's breastworks and surrendered.

CHAPTER XII

BATTLE AT YAZOO CITY

Midwinter—Through the Swamps—Gunboat Patrols—
Crossing the Mississippi—Through the Ice—Ferrying Guns—
Hardships—Engagement at Yazoo City—Harrying Sherman—
Under Suspicion—A Practical Joke—Battle at Yazoo City—
Casualties—A Social Call—Eastwood—Drowning Accident—A
Military Survey.

THE early days of January, 1864, found us floun-
dering through the swamps in an effort to deliver to
the trans-Mississippi department a lot of small arms,
rifles, and bayonets. General Stephen D. Lee, commander of the cavalry in our department, wrote General Ross that there had been two or three unsuccessful efforts to put two thousand stands of arms
across the Mississippi, and asking whether he thought
his command could put them over. General Ross
replied, " We will try." So the brigade started with
several wagons loaded with the arms and a battery
of four pieces. This January proved to be the coldest month of the war, and for downright acute suffering from exposure and privation probably no
month of our campaigning equalled this.

We crossed Yazoo River at Murdock's ferry, and
pretty soon were in Sunflower Swamp, about eight
miles across. A slow rain was falling and the weather
very threatening. With all the teams we had and
all the oxen that could be procured in the vicinity,
an all-day's job, we reached Sunflower with one lone

piece of artillery, every other wheeled vehicle being hopelessly bogged down in the swamp from two to five miles in our rear. While the command was crossing the river a blizzard swooped down upon us. By the time we reached a camp two miles beyond, icicles were hanging from our horses, and everything we possessed that was damp was freezing. The cold continued to increase, next morning everything was frozen stiff, and it would have been possible to skate on the ponds near the camps. In this state of affairs General Ross said to us: "What shall we do, give up the expedition or take these guns on our horses and carry them through?" The boys said: "Carry them through." We mounted and rode back to the river, left the horses on the bank and crossed in a ferryboat, where ensued a grand race for the wagons across the rough, frozen ground and ice, for on a fellow's speed depended the distance he would have to go for the load of guns he was to carry back to the horses. Warren Higginbothom, an athletic messmate of mine, passed me, and I asked him to save me some guns at the first wagon, which he did, and I returned to camp with other fortunate ones; but some of them were late in the night returning. So we remained in the same camp for another night. Many of the men were thinly clad and poorly shod for such a trip in the bitter cold weather, I myself being clad in a thin homespun gray jean jacket, without an overcoat; and having hung my gloves before the fire to dry and gotten them burned to a crisp, I was barehanded as well.

The next morning every man, including General Ross himself, took his quota of the guns, usually four apiece, and started to Gaines' ferry, Mississippi, about fifty miles distant. P through Bogue Folio Swamp about seven miles, ing the stream of that name and passing through the Deer Creek country, the garden spot of Mississippi, we came to within about three miles of the river and camped in a dry cypress swamp. As the river was closely patrolled by gunboats our aim was to cross the guns over at night. As no craft that a man could cross the river in was allowed to remain in the river, we found a small flatboat and dragged it with oxen over the frozen ground to the river, walking with loads of guns to meet it. The river here was running south and the cold north wind was coming down stream in almost a gale. The water was low and we approached it on a wide sandbar. Having slid the boat into the water, John B. Long, Nathan Gregg, of Company A, Si James, the Choctaw, and one other of the command volunteered to row it over. After it was well loaded with guns the boat was pushed off, but the strong wind drifted them down the river some distance, and, returning, they drifted down still farther, so that it was nine o'clock next morning when they returned to camp, with their clothes from their waists down covered with a sheet of ice so thick that they could not sit down. The first gunboat that passed destroyed the little flat. We then built another small boat, but before we could get it ready for use all the eddy portion of the river near the bank was frozen over and the current a mass of floating ice, so that it was impossible to cross in such a craft at night. Procuring two skiffs in addition to the boat, we crossed the remainder of the guns over in daylight, pushing through the floating ice with poles, the guns being delivered to Colonel Harrison's command on the west bank of the river. For the days and nights we were engaged in crossing these guns we lived on fresh pork found in the woods, eating this without salt, and a little corn parched in the ashes of our fires. The weather continued to grow colder, until the ice was four inches thick on the ponds. The guns being disposed of, the piece of artillery was run down to the bank of the river, when soon a small transport came steaming up the river. It was given one or two shots, when it blew a signal of distress and steamed to the opposite shore and landed, and was soon towed off by a large boat going up the river. With some of our men barefooted and many of them more or less frost-bitten we returned to Deer Creek, where we could get rations and forage. As for forage there were thousands of acres of fine corn ungathered, and we only had to go into the fields and gather what we wanted. The Federals had carried off the able-bodied negroes, and the corn was still in the fields, and along the creek and through the farms there were thousands and thousands of wild ducks. I am sure I saw more ducks at one glance than I had seen all my life before. We retraced our steps through the swamps and the cane-brakes and recrossed the Yazoo River in time to meet a fleet of twelve transports, loaded with white and black troops, escorted by two gunboats, ascending that river, evidently making for Yazoo City.

The Third Texas was sent out to meet a detachment of the enemy moving up the Mechanicsburg and

CAPTAIN H. L. TAYLOR
Commander Ross' Brigade Scouts

Yazoo City road, and drove them back towards Vicksburg, the rest of the brigade, in the meantime, fighting the river force at Satartia and Liverpool. The Third rejoined the brigade at Liverpool, but being unable to prevent the passage of the enemy, we moved rapidly up the river and beat them to Yazoo City. Placing our artillery in some earthworks thrown up by Confederates in the early part of the war, we formed a line of riflemen down at the water's edge. The fleet soon came steaming up the river, and when the front gunboat came opposite to us the battery began playing upon it, while the rifles kept their portholes closed so that they could not reply. It was not long before they abandoned the effort to land, dropped back and were soon out of sight down the river. Later in the day, from the smoke, we could see that they were steaming up Sunflower River, west of us.

When the people of Yazoo City saw that we had saved their town from occupation by negro troops, their gratitude knew no bounds, and this gratitude was shown practically by as great a hospitality, as was ever extended by any people to a command of Confederate soldiers. In the evening a squadron, including Company C, was left on picket below the city for the night, at the point occupied during the day, while the command moved out on the Benton road to camp. To the pickets during the evening the citizens sent out cooked provisions of the nicest and most substantial character, sufficient to have lasted them for a week.

The next morning the brigade returned and as everything remained quiet, with no prospect of an early return of the enemy's fleet, I rode uptown to take a view of the city. Numbers of others had done the same, and as the hour of noon approached we began to get invitations to dinner. Meeting a little white boy, he would accost you thus: " Mr. Soldier, Mamma says come and eat dinner with her." Next a little negro boy would run up and say: " Mr. Soldier, Mistis say come and eat dinner with her." And this manner of invitation was met on every corner, and between the corners. I finally accepted an invitation to dine with the family of Congressman Barksdale.

We were not allowed to enjoy the hospitality of this grateful city long on this visit, as General Sherman, who had planned a march to the sea, moved eastwardly out from Vicksburg, with a formidable force of infantry and artillery, and we were ordered to follow him. This we did, and kept his infantry closed up and his men from straggling. His cavalry, moving out from Memphis, was to form a junction with his main force at Meridian. Reaching that place, he halted, and we camped in the pine wood three or four miles north of the town. General Forrest was between us and the enemy's cavalry, and our object was to prevent a junction, thus defeating the purpose of the expedition, and if Forrest was unable to drive the cavalry back we were to go to his assistance—that is, Jackson's division was to do this.

One very cold, cloudy evening near sundown I was ordered to report to General Ross, mounted. When I reached headquarters I received verbal orders to proceed to Macon with the least possible delay, take charge of some couriers already there, use the telegraph, ascertain General Forrest's movements, and report from time to time by courier. The distance to Macon was, say, forty-five or fifty miles, and the way led mainly through forests, with a few houses on the road. Clad in my gray jean jacket, without overcoat or gloves, but well mounted and armed, I started, alone. Soon after dark a light snow began to fall and continued all night. About midnight I reached DeKalb, the county seat of Kemper County, where I spent half an hour in an effort to rouse somebody who could put me on the road to Macon. At daylight I was several miles from my destination. Stopping at a house for breakfast I lay down before the fire and slept while it was being prepared, and after breakfast finished my journey.

Approaching Macon from the south I crossed Noxubee River, spanned by a splendid covered bridge, and noticed that it was so filled with tinder that it easily might be fired if the Federal troops should come in sight. As I rode into the town and halted to make some inquiries, quite a number of citizens gathered around me to learn who I was, and ask for the news. One sympathetic old gentleman, seeing that my hands were bare and cold, stepped up and presented me with a pair of gloves. I found that the citizens were scared and excited, as they were situated between Sherman and his cavalry. I endeavored to allay their uneasiness, and advised them not to burn the bridge, even if the enemy should appear, as that would only cause a temporary delay, and would be a serious loss to the town and country. From this they concluded I was a spy in the interest of the enemy, as I learned later, and for a day or two my every movement was closely watched.

I now put up my horse, found my couriers, repaired to the telegraph office, and informed the operator of my instructions. I spent most of the time in the telegraph office, when late at night the operator told me of the suspicion that I was a spy, and that he had cleared it up by asking General Jackson over the wires who I was. After this, while on this duty, I was treated with great kindness.

General Jackson now moved up to re-enforce General Forrest, and I rejoined the command as it passed Macon. We moved up as far as Starkville, but, learning that the enemy's cavalry had been driven back, we returned to the vicinity of Meridian. As was expected, General Sherman began falling back towards Vicksburg, we following him. Arriving at Canton, Sherman, taking an escort, returned to Vicksburg, leaving his army to follow in command of General MacPherson. Under his command the Federal army moved without straggling and without further depredations. We learned from this improved condition of army discipline to respect MacPherson, and regretted to learn of his being killed in battle in front of Atlanta in July.

It was as the enemy returned on this trip that a battalion of Federal cavalry passed through Kosciusko, and their commander played a practical joke on the Union merchants there. These merchants, when they learned the Federals were coming, closed their doors and met them in the outskirts of town, and were loud in their assertions of loyalty to the

Union. The officer asked them if they had done anything for the Union they loved so much. " No," said they, " we have had no opportunity of doing anything, being surrounded by rebels as we are." " Well," said the officer, " we'll see. Maybe I can give you a chance to do a little something for the Union." Moving on uptown he found the rebels with open doors, and, in riding round, he would ask them why they had not closed up. They answered that they were so-called rebels, and were at the mercy of him and his men, and if their houses were to be plundered they did not wish the doors broken, and so they would offer no resistance. He placed guards in all the open doors, with instructions to permit no one to enter; then turning to his men, he told them if they could find anything they wanted in the houses that were closed, to help themselves, which they did. And thus an opportunity was given the " loyal " proprietors to do something for the Union.

Ross' brigade returned to Benton on the 28th of February, and was in the act of going into camps at Ponds, four miles down the plank road towards Yazoo City, when a squadron of negro cavalry from the city came in sight. General Ross ordered detachments of the Sixth and Ninth Texas to charge them. The negroes after the first fire broke in disorder and ran for dear life. The negro troops, a short time previous to this, had caught and murdered two of the Sixth Texas, and as these fellows were generally mounted on mules very few of them got back inside the breastworks, these few being mostly the white officers, who were better mounted than the negroes.   Among the killed along the road was found a negro that belonged to Charley Butts, of Company B, he having run away to join the First Mississippi Colored Cavalry.

On the evening of March 4 Brigadier-General Richardson, with his brigade of West Tennessee Cavalry, joined General Ross for the purpose of assisting in driving the enemy from Yazoo City, which is situated on the east bank of Yazoo River. The city with its surroundings was occupied by a force of about 2000 white and negro troops, commanded by Colonel James H. Coats, supported by three gunboats.   About eight o'clock on the morning of March 5, 1864, the city was attacked by Ross' and Richardson's brigades, Brigadier-General L. S. Ross in command.   Our fighting strength was about 1300 men, with two or three batteries; but as we dismounted to fight, taking out the horse-holders, every fourth man, this would reduce our fighting strength to about 1000 men.   The enemy had the advantage of several redoubts and rifle-pits, the main central redoubt being situated on the plank road leading from Benton to Yazoo City. We fought them nearly all day, and at times the fighting was terrific.   With the Third Texas in advance we drove in their pickets and took possession of all the redoubts but the larger central one.   This one was in command of Major George C. McKee, of the Eleventh Illinois Regiment with nine companies: about four companies of the Eighth Louisiana negro regiment; Major Cook, with part of his First Mississippi negro cavalry, the same that had murdered the two Sixth Texas men; and one piece

of artillery.   The Third and Ninth Texas and Fourteenth Tennessee cavalry found themselves confronting this redoubt.   Two of our batteries were placed
so as to obtain an enfilading fire at easy range, and
threw many shells into the redoubt, but failed to
drive the enemy out.   In the meantime General Richardson, with the rest of his brigade, the Sixth Texas
and the Legion, drove the remainder of the enemy's
forces entirely through the city to the protection
of their gunboats, and gained possession of the entire place except one or two brick warehouses near
the bank of the river, behind which their troops
had huddled near the gunboats.   The Sixth Texas
and Legion took position on the plank road in rear
of the large redoubt, and thus at four o'clock in
the afternoon we had it entirely surrounded, we
being in front some 150 yards distant.   At this
juncture General Ross sent Major McKee a flag of
truce and demanded an unconditional surrender.   The
firing ceased and the matter was parleyed over for
some time.   The first message was verbal, and Major
McKee declined to receive it unless it was in writing.
It was then sent in writing, and from the movements
we could see, we thought they were preparing to
surrender.   But they refused, owing perhaps to the
fact that General Ross declined to recognize the
negro troops as soldiers; and how they would have
fared at the hands of an incensed brigade of Texas
troops after they had murdered two of our men
in cold blood was not pleasant to contemplate.   As
for the negro troops,—well, for some time the
fighting was under the black flag—no quarter being asked or given.   Retaliation is one of the horrors

of war, when the innocent are often sacrificed for the inhuman crimes of the mean and bloodthirsty.

The parley in reference to surrendering being at an end, little more firing was indulged in, as both parties seemed to have grown tired of shooting at each other. The troops were under the impression that we were to assault the redoubt, but instead of doing so we quietly retired just before nightfall, and returned to our camp on the Benton road. This was explained by General Ross in his report in this way: "To have taken the place by assault would have cost us the loss of many men, more, we concluded, than the good that would result from the capture of the enemy would justify." Our loss in this engagement was: Ross' brigade, 3 killed and 24 wounded; Richardson's brigade, 2 killed and 27 wounded; total, 56. The enemy reported: 31 killed, 121 wounded, and 31 missing; total, 183.

Among our severely wounded was John B. Long, of Company C. Early in the day, ten o'clock perhaps, he was shot down on the skirmish line and was carried off the field and the word came down the line: "John B. Long is killed.—John B. Long is killed." This was heard with many regrets, as he was a favorite soldier in the command. This report was regarded as true by all of us at the front, until we returned to our camp. The next morning I found him in Benton, wounded in the head; unconscious, but not dead, and he is not dead to this day (August, 1899). The next morning all the enemy's forces left Yazoo City, and again Ross' brigade was regarded as an aggregation of great heroes by these good people.

One morning while we were camped in this neighborhood, one of the boys came to me with an invitation to visit a lady residing between our camps and Benton. She wished to see me because I had lived in Huntsville, Ala. When I called I found Mrs. Walker, daughter-in-law of General L. P. Walker, of Huntsville. She was a beautiful young woman, bright, educated and refined, easy and self-possessed in manner, and a great talker. She lived with her parents, Mr. and Mrs. Simpson, her husband being in the army. Mrs. Walker was an enthusiastic friend of the brigade, and would not admit that they had ever done anything wrong, and contended that, inasmuch as they had defended the city and county so gallantly, anything they needed or wanted belonged to them, and the taking it without leave was not theft. And this was the sentiment of many of these people.

For the remaining days of March we occupied practically the same territory we had been guarding from the fall of Vicksburg. On or about the last of March General Ross sent Colonel Dudley W. Jones, in command of the Third and Ninth Texas regiments, to attack the outpost of the force at Snyder's Bluff, destroy Yankee plantations, etc., etc. I did not accompany this expedition, I am sure, as I have no recollection of being with it; nor do I now remember why I did not do so. The Yankee plantations alluded to were farms that had been taken possession of by Northern adventurers, and were being worked under the shadow of the Federal army by slaves belonging to the citizens. Cotton being high, they expected to avail themselves of confiscated plantations and slaves to make fortunes raising cotton.   Colonel Jones captured and destroyed at least one such plantation, captured one hundred mules, some negroes, and also burned their quarters.

Early in April we started east, with the ultimate purpose of joining General Joseph E. Johnston's forces in Georgia, moving by easy marches.   There was some dissatisfaction among the men on account of heading our column toward the rising sun, as they had been promised furloughs on the first opportunity, and this looked like an indefinite postponement of the promised boon.   Arriving at Columbus, Miss., we rested, and here Lieutenant-General Leonidas Polk, then commanding the department, made a speech to the brigade, alluding to the fact that they had been promised furloughs, postponed from time to time, and assured us that as soon as the present emergency ended Ross' brigade should be furloughed.   He assured the men that he had the utmost confidence in their bravery and patriotism, and though it had been hinted to him, he said, that if he allowed these Texans to cross the Mississippi River they would never return, he entertained no such opinion of them.

We now moved from Columbus to Tuscaloosa, Ala., the former capital of that grand old State. The good people of this beautiful little city on the banks of the Black Warrior had never before seen an organized command of soldiers, except the volunteer companies that had been organized here and left the city and vicinity, and their terror and apprehensions when they learned that a brigade of Texans had arrived was amusing.   They would not have been in the least surprised if we had looted the town in twenty-four hours after reaching it. As we remained here several days, and went in and out of the city in a quiet orderly manner, they soon got over their fears. There were numbers of refugees here from Huntsville, Florence, and other north Alabama towns, and some of us found acquaintances, especially General Ross and his adjutant-general, Davis R. Gurley, who had been in college at Florence. During our stay the ladies gave several nice parties for the benefit of the brigade. While we were here a great many fish were being caught in a trap above the city, and the men would sometimes go at night in skiffs up to the trap and get the fish. On one occasion Lieutenant Cavin, Harvey Gregg, and a man named Gray, of Company A, went up, and getting their boat into a whirlpool, it was capsized and the men thrown out into the cold water, with overcoats and pistols on. Gregg and Gray were drowned and Cavin was barely able to get out alive.

After several days we moved some miles south of the city, where forage was more convenient. In the meantime General Loring, with his division, had come on from Mississippi. Receiving an invitation through Captain Gurley to attend a party given by a Florence lady to him and General Ross, I went up and spent two or three days in the city. While there I visited my friends in Loring's division, and also visited the State Lunatic Asylum, where I found in one of the inmates, Button Robinson, of Huntsville, a boy I had known for years. I also attended a drill of the cadets at the university. Friends of the two young men that were drowned had been

here dragging the river for their bodies for some
days, and finally they got one of General Loring's
batteries to fire blank cartridges into the water, and
their bodies rose to the surface, when they were taken
out and buried.

The mountainous country lying north of Tuscaloosa and south of the Tennessee valley was at this
time infested with Tories, deserters, " bushwhackers,"
and all manner of bad characters, and it was reported
that the Tories in Marion County were in open resistance. So on the morning of the 19th of April
Colonel D. W. Jones, of the Ninth, was sent with
detachments of the Sixth and Ninth Texas and a
squadron from the Third, under Captain Lee,
amounting in all to about 300 men, up into that
county to operate against these Tories. On the
same morning I was ordered to take fifteen men of
Company C and accompany Lieutenant De Sauls,
of the Engineers' Corps, from Tuscaloosa, up the
Byler road to Decatur, on the Tennessee River, and
return by way of the old Robertson road, leading
through Moulton and Jasper to the starting point,
for the purpose of tracing out those roads to complete a military map then in preparation. Applying
to the quartermaster and commissary for subsistence
for my men and horses, I was instructed to collect
" tax in kind." We moved out in advance of Colonel
Jones' command. Our duties on this expedition ne-
cessitated our stopping at every house on the road
to obtain the numbers of the lands,—that is, the
section, township, and the range,—ascertain the
quarter section on which the house stood, learn the
names of all creeks, note all cross roads, etc., etc.

I subsisted the men and horses on tax in kind, which
I had to explain to the poor people in the mountains,
as they had never heard of the law. There was not
much produced in this country, and there were so
many lawless characters in the mountains that the
tax collectors were afraid to attempt to collect
the impost. The people offered me no resistance,
however, and to make the burden as light as possible
I would collect a little from one and a little from
another. I had the horses guarded every night,
but really had no trouble. I met with one misfortune,
much deplored by me, and that was the killing of
James Ivey by Luther Grimes, but under circumstances that attached no blame to Grimes in the
eyes of those who saw the occurrence, as Ivey made
the attack and shot Grimes first, inflicting a scalp
wound on the top of his head. I reported the facts
when I reached the command, and there was never
any investigation ordered.

CHAPTER XIII

UNDER FIRE FOR ONE HUNDRED DAYS

Corduroy Breeches—Desolate Country—Conscript Headquarters—An "Arrest"—Rome, Ga.—Under Fire for One Hundred Days—Big and Little Kenesaw—Lost Mountain—Rain, Rain, Rain—Hazardous Scouting—Green Troops—Shelled—Truce—Atlanta—Death of General MacPherson—Ezra Church—McCook's Retreat—Battle Near Newnan—Results.

WE reached General Roddy's headquarters near Decatur, on Saturday, and rested until Monday noon. Starting back we passed through Moulton, were caught in a cold rain, sheltered our horses under a gin-shed, and slept in the cotton seed without forage or rations. Next morning I instructed the men to find breakfast for themselves and horses, and meet me at Mr. Walker's, down on the road. Taking De-Sauls and one or two others, I went on to Mr. Walker's, a well-to-do man, who owned a mill, where I hoped to get breakfast and some rations and forage to carry us across the mountain. Arriving at Walker's, he came out to the gate and I asked him first about forage and rations to take with us, and he said we could get them. Leaving DeSauls to question him about his land, I sought the lady of the house to arrange for breakfast. I found her very willing to feed us, as we were from eastern Texas, and knew of her father, who lived in Rusk County. Now De-Sauls was a resident of New Orleans, was dressed in a Confederate gray jacket and cap, and wore a

190

pair of corduroy trousers. Soon after the lady left the front room to have breakfast prepared, De-Sauls came in with a fearful frown on his face and said to me: " Barron, don't you think that d———d old scoundrel called me a Yankee? " " Oh," said I, " I guess he was joking." Just at this time Mr. Walker came up, looking about as mad as DeSauls, and said, " No, I am not joking. I believe you are *all* Yankees; look at them corduroy breeches! There hasn't been a piece of corduroy in the South since the war began, without a Yankee wore it." I treated the matter as a joke at first, until finding that the old gentleman was in dead earnest, I undertook to convince him that he was wrong, but found it no easy matter. Finally I asked him the distance to Huntsville? Forty miles. Then through my familiarity with the people and country in and around Huntsville I satisfied him that he was wrong, and then we were treated kindly by him and his family.

After leaving Tennessee valley we passed through the most desolate country I ever saw. For more than a day's march I found but one or two houses inhabited, and passing through the county seat of Winston County I was unable to find any person to tell me the road to Jasper. Arriving at Tuscaloosa I learned that Colonel Jones had returned and that the brigade had gone to Georgia, and I followed it, passing through Elyton, Blountsville, Talledega, and Blue Mountain. Camping one night at Blountsville, I met my friend Bluford M. Faris, formerly of Huntsville. Arriving at Talledega, I determined to spend one day, Saturday, there in order to have some shoeing done. This was conscript headquarters for

192 THE LONE STAR DEFENDERS

a large area of country, with a major commanding, and there was post-quartermaster, commissary, a provost marshal, and all the pomp and circumstance of a military post. I thought at one time I would have some trouble, but fortunately I came out all right.

In the first place I camped in a grove of timber convenient to water, but soon received a message from the commander that I had camped near his residence, and would I move somewhere else? He did not want men to depredate upon his premises. I replied that I would make good every depredation my men committed, and that it was not convenient for me to move. I was busy for some time in procuring rations, forage, and an order for horse-shoeing, and about the time I had these matters arranged I got a message requesting me to come to the provost marshal's office. On my way I saw my men out in line of battle near the court-house, with guns loaded and capped. Calling one of them to me, I learned that one or two of them had gone into the provost's office and he had cursed them as d———d stragglers belonging to a straggling brigade, and they gave him back some rough words, whereupon he had threatened to arrest them, and they were waiting to be arrested. Coming to the office I found the man in charge was a deputy. Introducing myself, I inquired what he wanted. He said some of my men had been to his office and cursed him, and he had threatened to arrest them and wished to know if I could control them. I told him I could control them as easily as I could control that many little children, but if he wished to arrest any of them, the men were just out there and he might send his men out to attempt it—if he could. I asked him what provocation he had offered, and made him acknowledge that he had called them " stragglers." I then told him they were not stragglers, but good soldiers and, besides, they were all gentlemen, and if he had not first insulted them they would have treated him in a gentlemanly way; that if he wished to deal with them to proceed, otherwise I would take charge of them. Oh, no, he did not wish to have any trouble. If I was willing for my men to take a drink, I had his permission, and the poor fellow was more than willing to turn the " stragglers " over to me. I called them all up, accompanied them to a saloon, and told them that those who wished it could take a drink. We then went about our business without further trouble.

From Talladega I proceeded to Blue Mountain, intending to go from there to Rome, but learning that our army was gradually falling back, and being unable to learn its position or when I could safely calculate on striking it in the flank, I turned my course southward, passed through Carrolton, crossed the Chattahoochee River, followed the river up to Campbellton, recrossed it and found my command fighting near new New Hope church on the —— day of May, 1864.

A detailed account of this campaign would make a large volume, and of course cannot be undertaken in these brief recollections. Our division of cavalry reached Rome, Ga., about the middle of May, and fought the Federal advance the same day, and then for one hundred days were under fire, with the exception that on two occasions we were ordered to follow cavalry raids sent to our rear. But for this brief respite we were under constant fire for this period, each day and every day. We were assigned a position on the extreme left of General J. E. Johnston's army, a position occupied by us during the entire campaigning, while General Joe Wheeler's cavalry was on the extreme right.

To give one day's duty is practically to give the duties of many other days. We always fought on foot. Sometimes behind breastworks, sometimes not, sometimes confronting infantry and sometimes cavalry. We would be up, have our horses equipped, form a line, detail horse-holders, and march to the front by daybreak, and take our position on the fighting line. About nine o'clock our cooked rations, consisting of one small pone of corn bread and three-eighths of a pound of bacon, was distributed to each man as we stood or lay in line of battle. While these rations would not have made a good hearty breakfast, they had to last us twenty-four hours. The skirmishing might be light or heavy, we might charge the enemy's works in our front, or we might be charged by them. Usually the musket-firing, and often artillery-firing, would be kept up until night, when leaving a skirmish line at the front, we would retire to our horses. We often changed position after night, which involved night marching, always changing in a retrograde movement. Sometimes the fighting would become terrific, for at times General Sherman would attack our whole line, miles and miles in length, and, under General Johnston these attacks were made with heavy loss to Sherman's army. Particularly was this the case in front of Big Kenesaw, Little Kenesaw, and Lost Mountain.

In this campaign the cavalry service was much harder than the infantry service. When night came on the infantry could fall down and sleep all night unless they had to change their position, while the cavalry were burdened with their horses. Marching back to our horses we hustled for all the forage the Government could furnish us, which was usually about one quart of shelled corn, and we were compelled to supplement this with something else, whatever we could find; sometimes it was oats, often green crab grass from the fields, and later, green fodder or pea vines. Often this gathering of horse feed lasted until ten or eleven o'clock, when the horses would be stripped and we could sleep, provided we were not to move.

Early in June it began to rain, and continued raining day and night for about twenty-five days, until the country was so boggy that it was almost impossible to move artillery or cavalry outside of the beaten roads. Sometimes when the rain was pouring down in torrents the enemy would be throwing shrapnels at us, and hundreds, perhaps thousands, of them without exploding, plunged into the soft earth and are doubtless there yet. During the rainy season there was a great deal of thunder and lightning, and artillery duels would occur either day or night, and sometimes it was difficult to distinguish between the thunder of heaven and the thunder of cannon and bursting shells. On one of those very rainy days we were in some timber south of a farm, while the enemy was in the timber north of it, only a few hundred yards distant, and had been firing at us in a pretty lively manner. General Ross sent for me and told me to go ascertain how far the enemy's line extended beyond our left. I mounted my horse and rode off, conning over in my mind the perplexing question as to how I was to gain the desired information, as the enemy in the thick woods could not be seen, and I could think of no other method than to ride into the field in view of their skirmishers, draw their fire and move on until the end of their line was apparent. Accordingly I rode into the open field and moved along some distance without being shot at; looking across the field near the opposite fence, I fancied I saw a line of skirmishers just inside of it, and tried in vain to attract their attention at long range. I rode back and forth, getting nearer to them all the time, until I got close enough to discover that the fancied pickets were black stumps, an illusion occasioned by the fact that a man in dark blue uniform on a rainy day looks black at a distance of two or three hundred yards. I was then worse puzzled than at first, for to go back and tell General Ross that I could not learn anything about their lines would never do. After a little hesitation I threw down the fence and rode into the thick undergrowth, expecting every minute to meet a volley of bullets. Going on some little distance I heard the word " Halt! " I halted, and was soon gratified to learn that I was confronting a small Confederate scouting party. Informing them of my object, they proposed showing me what I was looking for, and I was therefore able to return and report to my general, sound in body and much easier in mind.

During this long rainy spell we rarely slept two nights on the same ground and never had a dry blanket to sleep on. On the 3d day of July we fought General Schofield's Corps nearly all day, fighting and falling back (as they were pushing down a road leading to Sand Town, a crossing on the Chattahoochee River), passing through a line of breastworks on the crest of a ridge crossing the road at right angles, erected and occupied by the Georgia Militia, about the middle of the afternoon. As we passed into the breastworks one of our men was killed by a long-range ball. The militia had never been under fire and had never seen a man killed before. We were instructed to form a line immediately in their rear and rest, and to support them if the enemy should come; but beyond throwing a few shells over the works and skirmishing at long range, we had no farther trouble with the enemy that afternoon. Our men were very much amused at the sayings and doings of the militia at this time, but subsequently the Georgia militia were commanded by General G. W. Smith, an experienced officer, and after this they acted very gallantly in battle. They retired at night and we, leaving skirmishers in the works, went into camp. The next morning the Third Texas went into these breastworks, and while Captain Germany and myself were out in front deploying skirmishers he was severely wounded just below the knee, and was unfit for duty for several months.

General Schofield's Corps advanced in solid line of battle, and were allowed to take the works while

we fell back a short distance into the timber and
heard them give three cheers for Abe Lincoln, three
cheers for General Sherman and three cheers for
General Schofield! We then fought them again back
through the timber until we came to a lane leading
between farms across a little valley nearly a mile
wide. On the hill beyond was our infantry in breastworks, and just beyond the breastworks was the
narrow river bottom and Sand Town crossing, and
down in this little bottom were our horses. As we
entered the lane the enemy ran a battery up to the
edge of the timber and shelled us every step of the
way as we pulled through the long lane, tired and
dusty, about noon, that hot 4th of July. Passing
through the breastworks we mounted our horses in
a shower of shells and crossed the river. Here we
rested for twenty-four hours.

I went into Atlanta on the morning of the 5th,
and skirmishing across the river again began in the
afternoon. Here for some days we had a compara-
tively easy time, only picketing and skirmishing
across the river. As this seemed void of results, the
men on the north and south side of the river would
agree upon a truce and go in bathing together.
They would discuss the pending race for President
between Lincoln and McClellan. The Confederates
would trade tobacco for molasses and exchange newspapers, and when the truce was at an end each side
would resume its respective position, and the firing
would be renewed.

There continued to be more or less fighting north
of the river until July 9, when General Johnston
fell back into the defenses immediately in front of

Atlanta.   General Sherman's army also crossed the river and confronted General Johnston's lines near the city.   On or about the 19th General Johnston was superseded by General John B. Hood, and then began a series of hard battles around Atlanta, which were continued on the 20th, 21st, 22d, and other days, in which the losses on both sides were heavy. The Federal general, James B. MacPherson, was killed on the 22d.   On the 28th was fought the battle of Ezra Church.   On this day Companies C and D of the Third Texas were on picket in front of our command, and in the afternoon were driven back by overwhelming numbers, John B. Armstrong being slightly wounded and R. H. Henden very severely wounded.

We were soon met with orders to mount and move out to Owl Rock church on the Campbellton and Atlanta road, to assist Colonel Harrison, who was understood to be contending with General McCook's division of cavalry.   General McCook had crossed the river near Rivertown, not far from Campbellton, for the purpose of raiding in our rear, and General Stoneman, with another division, had simultaneously moved out around the right wing of our army.   The purpose was for these two commands to co-operate and destroy the railroad in our rear. General Wheeler's cavalry was sent after Stoneman. As General McCook had at least twelve hours the start of us we were unable to overtake him until afternoon of the next day.   In the meantime, before daylight, he struck the wagon train belonging to our division, burned ninety-two wagons and captured the teamsters, blacksmiths, the chaplain of the Third

Texas, and the inevitable squad that managed under all circumstances to stay with the train. We came up with McCook's command near Lovejoy Station, which is on the railroad thirty miles below Atlanta. We learned with joy that General Wheeler had overtaken Stoneman, captured him and a large portion of his command, and was able to come with a portion of his troops to assist in the operations against McCook. McCook now abandoned all effort to destroy railroad property, and began a retreat in order to get back into the Federal lines. We followed him until night when, as we had been in our saddles twenty-eight hours, we stopped, fed on green corn and rested a few hours. Some time before daylight next morning we mounted and moved on briskly. Early in the day we came close upon the enemy's rear and pressed them all day, during which time we passed scores of their horses, which from sheer exhaustion had been abandoned. Many of our horses, too, had become so jaded that they were unable to keep up.

About the middle of the afternoon, when near Newnan, the Federals stopped to give us battle. They had chosen a position in a dense skirt of timber back of some farms near the Chattahoochee River bottom, and here followed a battle which I could not describe if I would. I can only tell what the Third Texas did and sum up the general result. We were moved rapidly into the timber and ordered to dismount to fight. As many of our men were behind, instead of detailing the usual number of horse-holders, we tied the horses, leaving two men of the company to watch them. Almost immediately

LEONIDAS CARTWRIGHT

Company E, Third Texas Cavalry ; Member of
Taylor's Scouts, Ross' Brigade

FACING 200

we were ordered into line, and before we could be
properly formed were ordered to charge, through
an undergrowth so dense that we could only see a
few paces in any direction. As I was moving to my
place in line I passed John Watkins, who was to
remain with the horses, and on a sudden impulse I
snatched his Sharpe's carbine and a half dozen cartridges. On we went in the charge, whooping and
running, stooping and creeping, as best we could
through the tangled brush. I had seen no enemy in
our front, but supposed they must be in the brush or
beyond it. Lieutenant Sim Terrell, of Company F,
and myself had got in advance of the regiment, as it
was impossible to maintain a line in the brush, Terrell
only a few paces to my right. Terrell was an ideal
soldier, courageous, cool, and self-possessed in battle. Seeing him stop I did likewise, casting my eyes
to the front, and there, less than twenty-five yards
from me, stood a fine specimen of a Federal soldier,
behind a black jack tree, some fifteen inches in diam-
eter, with his seven-shooting Spencer rifle resting
against the tree, coolly and deliberately taking aim
at me. Only his face, right shoulder, and part of
his right breast were exposed. I could see his eyes
and his features plainly, and have always thought
that I looked at least two feet down his gun barrel.
As quick as thought I threw up the carbine and
fired at his face. He fired almost at the same instant and missed me. Of course I missed him, as
I expected I would, but my shot had the desired
effect of diverting his aim and it evidently saved
my life.

Directly in front of Terrell was another man,

whom Terrell shot in the arm with his pistol.   The
Federals both turned around and were in the act of
retreating when two or three of Terrell's men came
up and in less time than it takes to tell it two dead
bodies lay face downwards where, a moment before,
two brave soldiers had stood. I walked up to the
one who had confronted me, examined his gun, and
found he had fired his last cartridge at me.   Somehow I could not feel glad to see these two brave
fellows killed.   Their whole line had fallen back,
demoralized by the racket we had made, while these
two had bravely stood at their posts.   I have often
wondered what became of their remains, lying away
out in the brush thicket, as it was not likely that
their comrades ever looked after them.   And did
their friends and kindred at home ever learn their
fate?

We moved forward in pursuit of the line of dismounted men we had charged, and came in sight
of them only to see them retreating across a field.
Returning to our horses we saw them stampeding,
as Colonel Jim Brownlow, with his regiment of East
Tennesseans, had gotten among them, appropriated
a few of the best ones, stampeded some, while the
rest remained as we had left them.   We charged and
drove them away from the horses and they charged
us three times in succession in return, but each time
were repulsed, though in these charges one or two
of the best horses in the regiment were killed under
Federal riders.   These men were, however, only
making a desperate effort to escape, and were endeavoring to break through our lines for that purpose, as by this time General McCook's command

was surrounded and he had told his officers to get out the best they could. In consequence his army had become demoralized and badly scattered in their effort to escape. The prisoners they had captured, their ambulances, and all heavy baggage were abandoned, everything forgotten except the desire to return to their own lines. General Stoneman had started out with 5000 men and General E. M. McCook had 4000. Their objeect was to meet at Lovejoy Station, on the Macon Railroad, destroy the road, proceed to Macon and Andersonville and release the Federal prisoners confined at those two places. This engagement lasted about two hours, at the end of which we were badly mixed and scattered in the brush, many of the Confederates as well as Federals not knowing where their commands were.

General Ross summed up the success of his brigade on this expedition as follows: Captured, 587, including two brigade commanders, with their staffs; colors of the Eighth Iowa and Second Indiana; eleven ambulances, and two pieces of artillery. General Wheeler's men also captured many prisoners. Our loss on the expedition was 5 killed and 27 wounded. Among the wounded I remember the gallant Lieutenant Tom Towles, of the Third. The command now returned to its position in General Hood's line of battle, the prisoners being sent to Newnan, while I was ordered to take a sufficient guard to take care of them until transportation could be procured to send them to Andersonville. I had about 1250 enlisted men and 35 officers, who were kept here for several days. I confined them in a large brick warehouse, separating the officers from the privates by putting the officers in two rooms used for offices at the warehouse. I made them as comfortable as I could, and fed them well. I would turn the officers out every day into the front porch or vestibule of the warehouse, where they could get fresh air. They were quite a lively lot of fellows, except one old man, Colonel Harrison, I believe, of the Eighth Iowa. They appreciated my kindness and made me quite a number of small presents when the time came for them to leave.

This Newnan affair occurred July 30, 1864. General Hood had apparently grown tired of assaulting the lines in our front, and resumed the defensive. Our duties, until the 18th of August, were about the same as they had been formerly—heavy picketing and daily skirmishing. The casualties, however, were continually depleting our ranks: the dead were wrapped in their blankets and buried; the badly wounded sent to the hospitals in Atlanta, while the slightly wounded were sent off to take care of themselves; in other words, were given an indefinite furlough to go where they pleased, so that a slight wound became a boon greatly to be prized. Many returned to Mississippi to be cared for by some friend or acquaintance, while some remained in Georgia.

CHAPTER XIV

KILPATRICK'S RAID

Kilpatrick's Raid—Attack on Kilpatrick—Lee's Mill—Lovejoy's Station—The Brigade Demoralized—I Surrender—Playing 'Possum—I Escape—The Brigade Reassembles—Casualties.

On the night of August 18 Ross' brigade was bivouacked a short distance east of the road leading from Sand Town, on the Chattahoochee River, to Fairburn, on the West Point Railroad, eighteen miles west of Atlanta, thence to Jonesboro, on the Macon Railroad, some twenty miles south of Atlanta. This latter was the only railroad we then had which was of any material value to us, and we knew that General Sherman was anxious to destroy it, as an unsuccessful effort in that direction had been made only a few days previous.

We had a strong picket on the Sand Town and Fairburn road, and, as all was quiet in front, we "laid us down to sleep," and, perchance, to dream—of home, of the independence of the Confederate States, and all that was most dear to us. It was one of those times of fair promises, to the weary soldier, of a solid night's rest, so often and so rudely broken. Scarcely had we straightened out our weary limbs and folded our arms to sleep, when we were aroused by the shrill notes of the bugle sounding "boots and saddles." Our pickets were being driven in rapidly, and before we were in our saddles General Judson Kilpatrick, with a force of five thousand cavalry, with artillery, ambulances, pack mules and all else that goes to constitute a first-class cavalry raiding force, had passed our flank and was moving steadily down the Fairburn road. The Third Texas were directed to move out first and gain their front, to be followed by the other regiments of the brigade.

For the remainder of the night we moved as best we could down such roads as we could find parallel to Kilpatrick's line of march—so near, in fact, that we could distinctly hear the clatter of their horses' hoofs, the rumbling of their artillery, and the familiar rattle of sabers and canteens. Soon after daylight we came in sight of his column crossing the railroad at Fairburn, charged into it and cut it in two for the time. They halted, formed a line of battle, and we detained them in skirmishing until we managed to effect our object,—the gaining their front,—and during the day, until late in the afternoon, detained them as much as possible on their march.

Below Fairburn Kilpatrick's main column took the Jonesboro road, while a small column took the road leading to Fayetteville, a town about ten miles west of Jonesboro. Ross' brigade, continuing in front of the main column and that of Armstrong, followed the Fayetteville road. Just before night we passed through Jonesboro, which is ten or twelve miles from Fairburn, and allowed Kilpatrick to occupy the town for the night. Ross' brigade occupied a position south of the town near the railroad, while Armstrong was west; General Ferguson, whose brigade was numerically stronger than either of the others, being directed to go out on a road leading east. As we afterwards learned, they failed to find their road, or got lost, and, so far as I remember, were not heard from for a day or two. Thus posted, or intended to be posted, the understanding and agreement was that we should make a triangular attack on Kilpatrick at daylight the next morning.

Our brigade moved on time and marched into the town, only to learn that, with the exception of a few stragglers who had overslept themselves, not a Federal soldier was to be found. The brigade followed them eastwardly from Jonesboro, and in due time came up with their rear-guard at breakfast behind some railworks near Lee's Mill, and from this time until along in the afternoon we had a pretty warm time with their rear. They were moving on a road that intersects the McDonough and Lovejoy road, and when they struck this road they turned in the direction of Lovejoy Station.

We finally came up with the main force ensconced behind some heavy railworks on a hill near a farmhouse a short distance east of the station. We had to approach them, after leaving the timber, through a lane probably three-quarters of a mile in length. The farm was mostly uncultivated, and had been divided into three fields by two cross-fences, built of rails running at right angles with the lane, and these were thrown right and left to admit of the free passage of cavalry. In the eastern cross fence, however, a length some twenty or thirty yards, and but a few rails high, was left standing, when a ditch or ravine running along on the west side was too deep to be safely crossed by cavalry. In this lane the command dismounted, leaving the horses in the hands of holders, and deployed in line in the open field, to the left or south side of the lane, and a section of Croft's Georgia battery was placed on an elevation to the right of the lane.

I had been sent back to Lee's Mill to hurry up a detail left to bury one of our dead, so was behind when the line was formed. Having, on the day we fought McCook, picked up a mule for my boy Jake to ride, I now had him leading my horse to rest his back, while I rode the mule. I rode up and gave my rein to a horse-holder, and was hurrying on to join the line when they charged the railworks, and when I got up with them they had begun to fall back. The brigade, not having more than four hundred men for duty, was little more than a skirmish line. During the day General Hood had managed to place General Reynolds' Arkansas brigade at Lovejoy Station, which fact Kilpatrick had discovered, and while we were showing our weakness in an open field on one side, General Reynolds managed to keep his men under cover of timber on the other. Thus Kilpatrick found himself between an unknown infantry force in front and a skirmish-line of dismounted cavalry and a section of artillery in his rear. He concluded to get out of this situation—and he succeeded. Being repulsed in the charge on the railworks, by a heavy fire of artillery and small arms, we fell back and re-formed our line behind the first cross fence. Three regiments of the enemy then rapidly moved out from behind their works, the Fourth United States, Fourth Michigan, and Seventh

Pennsylvania, and charged with sabers, in columns of fours, the three columns abreast. As they came on us at a sweeping gallop, with their bright sabers glittering, it was a grand display. And Ross' brigade was there and then literally run over, trampled under foot, and, apparently annihilated. Just before the charge they had shelled our horses in the lane, which, consequently, had been moved back into the timber.

What could we do under the circumstances? If we had had time to hold a council of war and had deliberated over the matter ever so long, we would probably have acted just as we did; that is, acted upon the instinct of self-preservation, rather than upon judgment. No order was heard; not a word spoken; every officer and every man took in the whole situation at a glance: no one asked or gave advice: no one waited for orders. The line was maintained intact for a few seconds, the men emptying their pieces at the heads of the columns. This created a momentary flutter without checking their speed, and on they came in fine style. There was no time for reloading, and every one instinctively started for the horses a mile in the rear, a half mile of open field behind us, and all of us much fatigued with the active duties performed on the sultry summer day. Being very much fatigued myself and never being fleet of foot, I outran only two men in the brigade, Lieutenant W. H. Carr, of Company C, and W. S. Coleman, of Company A, of the Third Texas, who were both captured, and I kept up with only two others, Captain Noble and Lieutenant Soap, also of the Third Texas. We three came to the ravine already described, at the same instant. Soap dropped into

it, Noble jumped over and squatted in the sage grass
in the corner of the fence.   I instantly leaped the
ravine and the rail fence, and had gone perhaps ten
or fifteen steps when the clatter of horses' hoofs
became painfully distinct, and "Surrender, sir!"
rang in my ear like thunder.

Now, I had had no thought of the necessity of surrendering, as I had fondly hoped and believed I
would escape.   Halting, I looked up to ascertain
whether these words were addressed to me, and instantly discovered that the column directly in my
wake was dividing, two and two, to cross the ravine,
coming together again just in front of me, so that
I was completely surrounded.   This *was* an emergency.   As I looked up my eyes met those of a stalwart rider as he stood up in his stirrups, his drawn
saber glittering just over my head; and, as I hesi-
tated, he added in a kind tone: "That's all I ask
of you, sir."   I had a rifle in my hand which had
belonged to one of our men who had been killed near
me during the day.   Without speaking a word, I
dropped this on the ground in token of my assent.
"All right," said he, as he spurred his horse to overtake some of the other men.

Just at this time our artillery began throwing
shells across the charging columns, and the first one
exploded immediately above our heads, the pieces
falling promiscuously around in my neighborhood,
creating some consternation in their ranks.   Taking
advantage of this, I placed my left hand above my
hip, as if struck, and fell as long a fall as I could
towards the center of the little space between the
columns, imitating as best I could the action of a

mortally wounded man,—carefully falling on my right side to hide my pistol, which I still had on. Here I lay, as dead to all outward appearances as any soldier that fell during the war, and remained in this position without moving a muscle, until the field was clear of all of Kilpatrick's men who were able to leave it. To play the rôle of a dead man for a couple of hours and then make my escape may sound like a joke to the inexperienced, and it was really a practical joke on the raiders; but to me, to lie thus exposed on the bare ground, with a column of hostile cavalry passing on either side all the time, and so near me that I could distinctly hear any ordinary conversation, was far from enjoyable. I am no stranger to the hardships of a soldier's life; I have endured the coldest weather with scant clothing, marched day after day and night after night without food or sleep; have been exposed to cold, hunger, inclement weather and fatigue until the power of endurance was well-nigh exhausted, but never did I find anything quite so tedious and trying as playing dead. I had no idea of time, except that I knew that I had not lain there all night. The first shell our men threw after I fell came near killing me, as a large piece plowed up the ground near enough to my back to throw dirt all over me. Their ammunition, however, was soon exhausted, the guns abandoned, and that danger at an end.

As things grew more quiet the awful fear seized me that my ruse would be discovered and I be abused for my deception, and driven up and carried to prison. This fear haunted me until the last. Now, to add to the discomfort of my situation, it began to rain, and never in my life had I felt such a rain. When in my fall I struck the ground my hat had dropped off, and this terrible rain beat down in my face until the flesh was sore. But to move an arm or leg, or to turn my face over for protection was to give my case completely away, and involved, as I felt, the humiliation of a prison life; than which nothing in the bounds of probability in my life as a Confederate soldier was so horrible, in which there was but one grain of consolation, and that was that I would see my brother and other friends who had been on Johnson's Island for some months.

The last danger encountered was when some dismounted men came near driving some pack mules over me. Finally everything became so quiet that I ventured to raise my head, very slowly and cautiously at first, and as not a man could be seen I finally rose to my feet. Walking up to a wounded Pennsylvania cavalryman I held a short conversation with him. Surveying the now deserted field, so lately the scene of such activity, and supposing as I did that Ross' brigade as an organization was broken up and destroyed, I was much distressed. I was left alone and afoot, and never expected to see my horse or mule any more, which in fact I never did, as Kilpatrick's cavalry, after charging through the field, had turned into the road and stampeded our horses.

I now started out over the field in the hope of picking up enough plunder to fit myself for service in some portion of the army. In this I succeeded beyond my expectation, as I found a pretty good, completely rigged horse, only slightly wounded, and a pack-mule with pack intact, and I soon loaded the mule well with saddles, bridles, halters, blankets, and oil cloths. Among other things I picked up a Sharp's carbine, which I recognized as belonging to a messmate. While I was casting about in my mind as to what command I would join, I heard the brigade bugle sounding the assembly! Sweeter music never was heard by me. Mounting my newly-acquired horse and leading my pack-mule, I proceeded in the direction from which the bugle notes came, and on the highest elevation in the field, on the opposite side of the lane, I found General Ross and the bugler. I told my experience, and heard our gallant brigadier's laughable story of his escape. I sat on my new horse and looked over the field as the bugle continued to sound the assembly occasionally, and was rejoiced to see so many of our men straggling in from different directions, coming apparently out of the ground, some of them bringing up prisoners, one of whom was so drunk that he didn't know he was a prisoner until the next morning.

Near night we went into camp with the remnant collected, and the men continued coming in during the night and during all the next day. To say that we were crestfallen and heartily ashamed of being run over is to put it mildly; but we were not so badly damaged, after all. The horse-holders, when the horses stampeded, had turned as many as they could out of the road and saved them. But as for me, I had suffered almost a total loss, including the fine sword that John B. Long had presented me at Thompson's Station, and which I had tied on my saddle. My faithful Jake came in next morning, and although he could not save my horse, he had saved himself, his little McCook mule and some of my soldier clothes. My pack-mule and surplus rigging I now distributed among those who seemed to need them most.

Including officers, we had eighty-four or eighty-five men captured, and only sixteen or eighteen of these were carried to Northern prisons. Among them were seven officers, including my friend Captain Noble, who was carried to Johnson's Island, and messed with my brother until the close of the war. Captain Noble had an eye for resemblances. When he first saw my brother he walked up to him and said, " I never saw you before, but I will bet your name is Barron, and I know your brother well." The other prisoners who escaped that night and returned to us next day included my friend Lieutenant Soap, who brought in a prisoner, and Luther Grimes, owner of the Sharp's carbine, already mentioned, who had an ugly saber wound in the head. I remember only two men of the Third Texas who were killed during the day—William Kellum of Company C, near Lee's Mill; and John Hendricks, of Company B, in the charge on the railworks. These two men had managed to keep on details from one to two years, being brought to the front under orders to cut down all details to increase the fighting strength, and they were both killed on the field the first day they were under the enemy's fire.

Among the wounded was Captain S. S. Johnson, of Company K, Third Texas, gunshot wound, while a number of the men were pretty badly hacked with sabers. Next day General Ross went up to General Hood's headquarters and said to him: " General, I got my brigade run over yesterday." General Hood replied, " General Ross, you have lost nothing by that, sir. If others who should have been there had been near enough to the enemy to be run over, your men would not have been run over." This greatly relieved our feelings, and the matter became only an incident of the campaign, and on the 22d day of August Ross' brigade was back in its position ready for duty.

CHAPTER XV

UNION SOLDIER'S ACCOUNT OF KILPATRICK'S RAID

Kilpatrick's Raid—Ordered to the Front—Enemy's Artillery Silenced—We Destroy the Railroad—Hot Work at the Railroad—Plan of Our Formation—Stampeding the Horses—The Enemy Charges—Sleeping on Horseback—Swimming the River—Camped at Last.

AFTER the war ended I made a friend of Robert M. Wilson of Illinois, who served in the Fourth United States Cavalry, and he kindly wrote out and sent me his account of this raid, and by way of parenthesis I here insert it, as it may be of interest.

" The following is an account of the Kilpatrick raid, made in August, 1864, written partly from memory and partly from a letter written August 28, 1864, by Captain Robert Burns, acting assistant adjutant-general of the First Brigade, Second Cavalry Division, I acting as orderly for him part of the time on the raid. I was detailed at brigade headquarters as a scout during the Atlanta campaign and until General Wilson took our regiment as his escort. On the 17th of August, 1864, at one o'clock, A. M., ours and Colonel Long's Brigade (the First and Second), of Second Cavalry Division, all under the command of Colonel Minty, left our camp on Peach Tree Creek, on the left of our army northeast of Atlanta, at seven o'clock next morning; reported to General Kilpatrick at Sand Town on the right of our army, having during the night passed from one end or flank of our army to the other.   We remained at Sand Town until sundown of the 18th, when we started out to cut the enemy's communications south of Atlanta.   Two other expeditions, Stoneman's and McCook's, well equipped, before this had been ruined in attempting the same thing.   We, however, imagined we were made of sterner stuff, and started off in good spirits.   The command consisted of Third Cavalry Division (Kilpatrick's), under Colonel Murray, about 2700 men, and two brigades of our division (the Second), under command of Colonel Minty, about 2700 men also—the whole commanded by Kilpatrick (or Kill Cavalry, as we always called him).

"Away we went, Third Division in advance.   The night was a beautiful moonlight one, and we would have enjoyed it more if we had not been up all the night preceding.   We did not go more than three miles before we ran into the enemy's pickets, when we had to go more slowly, driving them before us, dismounting to feel the woods on both sides, etc., etc. Consequently it was morning when we reached the Atlanta & West Point Railroad near Fairburn.   At Red Oak we had torn up about half a mile of the track when the rear battalion of Seventh Pennsylvania Cavalry was suddenly attacked by a force of dismounted men and artillery.   Just back of where our column was struck were the ambulances, the darkies leading officers' horses, pack-mules, etc., etc. Several shells dropped among them, and they thought the kingdom had come, sure.   The Fourth United States Cavalry, being in rear of the ambulances, soon

drove the enemy away.   All this time the head of the
column kept moving on, as time was precious and we
could not stop for slight scrimmages.

"General Kilpatrick, not being satisfied with the
progress made by his advance, ordered our brigades
to take the front and Murray the rear.   (We had
learned before starting that it was expected we, our
division, would do all the fighting.)   Long's brigade,
in advance, had not gone more than half a mile when
he found a strong force of the enemy in his front.
He had to dismount his men to drive the enemy from
the rail barricades they had made, but he would find
them in the same position half a mile farther on.
Long kept his men dismounted, having number four
lead the horses.   I was close up with the advance
with Colonel Minty.   We drove the enemy steadily
but slowly back, until we came to the valley through
which Flint River runs, when they were reinforced by
Ferguson's brigade of cavalry (we had been fighting Ross' brigade thus far), and opened on us
sharply with artillery when we commenced descend-
ing the hill, the shells and bullets rattling lively
around us.   Two guns of our battery—we had with
us four guns of Chicago Board of Trade which belonged to our division, and Murray had with him
four guns of the Eleventh Wisconsin Battery—
were soon brought up and succeeded in silencing the
enemy's artillery, the first striking an artilleryman
and blowing him to pieces.   Our division were then
all dismounted and moved forward at the double-
quick under fire of our eight guns, and drove the
enemy clear through Jonesboro, crossing the bridge
on the stringer.   Our brigade (First) had the ad-

vance, being nearly all deployed as skirmishers. We then seized the railroad for which we had started, and we commenced to smash things generally. The track was torn up for about two miles, the depot and public buildings burned, and destruction was let loose. While this was going on the enemy returned to the attack, and our division was sent to meet them, the Third Division turning the rails. The enemy were driven southward and we were pushed that way, to shove them farther back. Before was darkness and death, behind the burning buildings and smoking ruins, and now it also began to thunder, lightning, and pour down rain in torrents. All this time General Kilpatrick had one of his bands behind us playing " Yankee Doodle " and other patriotic airs. It appeared as if defeat was coming, for we could hear the whistle of the cars in front of us and knew that the enemy were being reinforced from below. We then determined to flank them, so about midnight our brigade, followed by the Third Division, moved in a southeasterly direction about seven miles, Long's brigade being left to cover the rear.

" When seven miles out we stopped to feed, close to 6 A. M., about a mile from Murray's Division, but were little protected, as both hills were cleared and the valley had but few trees in it. Our brigade was ordered to mount and move forward when Colonel Long's brigade was attacked by the cavalry that followed us from Jonesboro. The enemy's forces consisted of the brigades of Ross, Ferguson, and Armstrong, about 4500 men. Our brigade moved on and turned sharply to the right, in a southwesterly direction, to strike the railroad again about eight

miles below Jonesboro. I stayed on the hill with
Captain Burns, for a short time, to witness the
skirmishing between Long and the enemy. From
where we were all our maneuvers could be distinctly
seen, as also the enemy, who would advance upon our
men, only to be driven back. It was a beautiful
sight. 'By Heaven, it was a noble sight to see—
by one who had no friend or brother there:'

"Captain Burns, myself following, now galloped
off to overtake our brigade, which we soon did. Colonel Long had orders to follow as quickly as possible,
Colonel Murray to come after. We (our brigade)
pushed for Lovejoy Station. When within a mile
and a half of the railroad we halted for the rest of
the command to join us. About a mile from the
railroad the road forks, the two prongs striking the
railroad about a half a mile apart. A few hundred
feet in front of and parallel to the railroad another
road ran. The Fourth Michigan was sent by the
right-hand road to the railroad, which it reached
without any trouble; the rest of the brigade took the
left-hand prong of the road, having for the last mile
or two been driving off about a dozen cavalrymen. As
we neared the railroad the firing became hotter and
hotter. The Seventh Pennsylvania Cavalry was dismounted and sent forward to the woods—one battalion, four companies, of it had been advance
guard. Hotter grew the firing, and the horses of
the advance who had dismounted came hurrying
back. The Fourth United States (Regulars) were
then dismounted and sent in. Captain Burns was
sent back to hurry up two of Long's regiments, but
before this could be done the Seventh Pennsylvania

and Fourth Regulars were driven from the woods in some confusion. We had run on a brigade of infantry who were lying in the woods behind barricades at the side of the railroad, and a force of the enemy was also pushed in on the right, where the Fourth Michigan were at work. Long's brigade was put in position to check the advancing Confederates, and our battery brought up, as the woods in front and on our left were swarming with the enemy, and the Fourth Regulars and Seventh Pennsylvania were placed in support of the battery. Poor fellows, they were badly cut up!

"One of Long's regiments was formed near the fork of the road, the Fourth Michigan was being placed there, and the enemy tried again and again to take our battery. It fought magnificently, and the guns were made to radiate in all directions and did splendid work, our men supporting them well. One of the guns, by the rebound, had broken its trail off short, so that it could not be drawn from the field. When the rest of the pieces had been withdrawn Colonel Minty called for men to draw off the piece by hand. Captain Burns took about twenty men of the Fourth Michigan Cavalry down and helped pull it off, though the enemy were very close to us. While this was taking place, heavy firing was heard in our rear, for the cavalry with which we had been fighting had followed us, and had us in a pretty tight box, as follows: a brigade of infantry in our front and partly on our left; a division moving on our right and but a short distance off; three brigades of cavalry in our rear. Stoneman and McCook threw up the sponge under like circumstances. We de-

cided we must leave the railroad alone, and crush the
enemy's cavalry, and consequently withdrew from
fighting the infantry, who now became very quiet,
probably expecting to soon take us all in.

" The command was faced to the rear as follows:
Our brigade was formed on the right hand side of the
road, each regiment in columns of fours (four men
abreast) ; the Fourth Regulars on the left; Fourth
Michigan center; Seventh Pennsylvania on the right,
Long's brigade formed in close columns with regimental front, that is, each regiment formed in line,
the men side by side, boot to boot, thus:

MINTY'S BRIGADE

FOURTH U. S.	FOURTH MICH.	SEVENTH PENN.
o o o o	o o o o	o o o o
o o o o	o o o o	o o o o
o o o o	o o o o	o o o o
o o o o	o o o o	o o o o
o o o o	o o o o	o o o o

LONG'S BRIGADE

FIRST OHIO

o o o o o o o o o o o o o o o o o o

THIRD OHIO

o o o o o o o o o o o o o o o o o o o

FOURTH OHIO

o o o o o o o o o o o o o o o o o o o o

" The last regiment was deployed in rear of the
others so as to take in a large space of ground and
pick up prisoners and trophies.   You see, we were to
break through the enemy, smashing them, and Long
was to sweep over the ground and pick them up.
This was soon determined on, for there was no time
to lose.   A few of our men were in front of us, dismounted, skirmishing with the enemy, and they were
told to throw down the fence where they were.   The
enemy all this time was keeping them engaged as
much as possible, while a large force of them were
building rail barricades.   We were formed just below the brow of the hill, skirmishers on the crest of
it, the enemy's artillery to our left and front playing over us, and bullets and shells flying thick over
our heads.   We drew saber, trotted until we came to
the crest of the hill and then started at a gallop.
Down the hill we went, the enemy turning canister
upon us, while the bullets whistled fiercely, and the
battery away on our right threw shells.   We leaped
fences, ditches, barricades, and were among them,
the artillery being very hot at this time.   You could
almost feel the balls as they passed by.   The Fourth
Michigan and Seventh Pennsylvania went straight
forward to the woods, the field over which they passed
being at least a half a mile wide, with three fences,
one partially built barricade, and a number of ditches
and gullies, some very wide and deep.   Of course
many of the men were dismounted, and upon reaching the woods they (our men) could not move fast,
and they turned to the right and joined the main
column in the road about one and a half miles from
the start.   The Fourth Regulars (my regiment, as

I joined it when the charge was ordered) could not keep parallel with the rest of the brigade on account of high fences in our front, and seeing an opening in the fence we turned to the left, and struck out on the main road, coming upon the enemy in the road near their battery, and sending them flying. We were soon among the led horses of the dismounted men in their rear and among the ambulances, and a perfect stampede took place, riderless horses and ambulances being scattered in all directions, we in the midst of them, shooting and cutting madly. A part of our regiment, with some of the Fourth Michigan and Seventh Pennsylvania, dashed at the battery, drove the men from the pieces, and captured three of the guns. Private William Bailey, a young Tennessean from near McMinnville, who belonged to Fourth Michigan Cavalry (he was associated with me at headquarters as scout), shot the captain. We brought away the guns, and the charge continued for about two miles, when we halted for the command to close up. Colonel Long's brigade did not charge in line as it was intended, for, finding that the ground was impracticable, it formed in column and followed the Fourth Regulars. Colonel Murray's command, instead of sweeping all to the left, as we supposed they would do, turned to the right and followed Long. Had Murray done what was expected, both sides of the road would have been cleaned out.

"Immediately after the charge and while we were pushing through the woods it commenced to rain, and poured in torrents. The command was now started for McDonough, but before the whole of it had moved off, Long's brigade, which had been moved to cover the rear, was fiercely attacked by the infantry of the enemy. Colonel Long fought them for about two hours, when, his ammunition giving out, he was obliged to retire. (Here Long was wounded twice.) The Fourth Michigan and Seventh Pennsylvania were formed in the rear, Long behind rail barricades which had been hastily thrown up. The Fourth United States Regulars being out of ammunition were sent on to McDonough, where the Ninety-second Illinois Mounted Infantry divided ammunition with some of us near this town. One of Long's regiments assisted the Fourth Michigan and Seventh Pennsylvania. Long passed his men through when the enemy came on us. Then we had it hot and heavy, the enemy charging several times, but were repulsed. All this fighting here was done dismounted, and was for the purpose of holding back the enemy until our main column could get out of the way. Our battery (three pieces) during this fight burst one gun and wedged another, getting a shell part way down it, so it could not be moved either way, so we had one gun only, but that was used with effect, the enemy meanwhile playing their artillery into our columns all along the road. You see our two brigades had to do all the fighting, lead the charge, and cover the retreat. As soon as our men had passed on about a mile, our rear-guard followed, and we were not molested again. We pushed slowly on to McDonough, crossed Walnut Creek, and near morning lay down in the mud for sleep. How tired we were I cannot tell, and men would tumble prone from their horses, and it was next to impossible to

226 THE LONE STAR DEFENDERS

awaken them. Frequently two or three men would
fall asleep upon their horses, who would stop, and
the whole column behind them would naturally do the
same, too, supposing that there was obstruction
ahead. Hundreds of men were sometimes asleep in
that way upon their horses in the mud for an hour
or so at a time. During this time I fell asleep for
about two hours, and awoke drenched to the skin,
for it was raining, and fearfully dark and very dis-
agreeable. About two o'clock we found a place to
stop. I never before that knew what fatigue meant,
for I had not slept a wink for the nights of the 17th,
18th, 19th, and 20th until the morning (about 2
A. M.) of the 21st, except what I had when riding
along. We had had but three meals, and but little
time to eat them, had fought seven pretty hard
fights, besides skirmishing, etc., etc. At daybreak
the next morning we started on again. At Cotton
River the bridge was gone, the stream much swollen
by rain, so that it could not be forded and the horses
were obliged to swim it. As the current was very
swift, we had a terrible time crossing it. We, our
brigade, lost one man and about sixty horses drowned
here, and nearly all our pack-mules also. We could
not get the wagon with the two disabled guns across
at all, and rumor said they were buried here, and the
site marked as the graves of two soldiers of the
Fourth United States Cavalry. It was terrible to
see the poor wounded carried across, some fastened
on horses, while others were taken over in ambulances. We all finally got over, but if the enemy
had pushed us here most of the command would have
been captured. We were now nearly all out of am-

G. A. McKee

Private Company C, Third Texas Cavalry

munition, and many an anxious glance I gave to the rear, it being a relief when all were over. We then crossed South River bridge, burning all the bridges for ten miles each side, and camped that night at Lithonia. The next day we returned to our camp at Peach Tree Creek, having made a complete circuit of the two armies of Hood and Sherman. We did not do all we hoped we could when we started, but *we did all we could.* Notwithstanding what we had suffered, General Sherman was much dissatisfied with us, expecting more from us than lay in our power (or his either) to accomplish.

" In the above narrative I have drawn very largely from a letter written August 28, 1864, by Captain Burns (as stated before), printed in a work called ' Minty and the Cavalry,' though about all I have written occurred under my own observation. We captured three stands of colors claimed to belong to the Third Texas Cavalry,* Zachariah Rangers, and Benjamin's Infantry.

" Our aggregate loss in First and Second Brigades, killed, wounded, and missing, was 14 officers, 192 men." †

" ROBERT M. WILSON,
" Company M, Fourth United States Cavalry."

* If the Third Texas colors were captured by them, they were found in an ambulance, as we did not have the flag unfurled on this expedition.

† It will be noted here that the aggregate loss of 206 men is only the loss of one division, not including Kilpatrick's Division and the two batteries.

CHAPTER XVI

CLOSE OF THE ATLANTA CAMPAIGN

Sherman Changes His Tactics—Hood Deceived—Heavy
Fighting—Atlanta Surrenders—End of the Campaign—Losses
—Scouting—An Invader's Devastation—Raiding the Raiders—
Hood Crosses the Coosa—A Reconnoissance—Negro Spies—
Raiding the Blacks—Crossing Indian Creek—A Conversion.

GENERAL SHERMAN had been impatient and dissatisfied that his cavalry was unable to destroy the
Macon or Brunswick Railroad, and now changed his
tactics. He had been in front of Atlanta, since General Hood had been in command, a period of about
five weeks. In a few days after Kilpatrick's return,
he began withdrawing his forces from the front of
that beleaguered city, crossed to the north side of
the Chattahoochee, marched his main force down to
Sand Town, recrossed the river, and moved directly
on Jonesboro, some twenty miles below Atlanta.

I do not believe, and never have believed, that General Hood understood this maneuver until it was too
late to save even his stores, arms, and ammunition in
Atlanta. His infantry scouts, it was understood and
believed at the time, watched the enemy's movements,
to the point of their crossing to the north side of
the Chattahoochee, and reported that they were retreating, while our cavalry scouts reported that they
were recrossing at Sand Town, in heavy force in
our front.

We, that is, our cavalry, began fighting the head

of their column as soon as they crossed the river, and fought them for detention and delay, as best we could, all the way to the Flint River Crossing near Jonesboro, just as we had fought Kilpatrick's force a few days before. General Hood, being advised that a heavy force of infantry and artillery was moving on Jonesboro, sent a portion of his army down there, and they fought the enemy most gallantly, but it seemed to me that our army should have been in their front long before they crossed Flint River. As it was, General Sherman threw his army across the railroad, on the first day of September, between us and Atlanta, and, while the fighting was terrific, we were unable to drive them off. A terrible battle, in which there were no breastworks, was fought late in the evening, and General Cleburne's division was cut in two, for the first time during the war, when General Govan of his division was captured and Colonel Govan killed. We were in line, dismounted, just on General Cleburne's right, forming a mere skirmish line, in order to cover the enemy's front. The welcome shades of night soon gathered around us, and the fighting ceased when the opposing lines were almost together. I was on picket two or three hundred yards back of the enemy's line until one or two o'clock in the morning. All this time they were felling timber and strengthening their position for the fighting they expected in the morning. During the evening Lieutenant-Colonel Berry of the Ninth Texas Cavalry was killed.

Soon after midnight a courier from General Hood passed us and informed us that Atlanta was given up. As soon as he reached our headquarters a courier was sent to order us to fall back.   And thus ended the last battle of the long campaign about Atlanta, a campaign involving continuous fighting for three and a half months.

Very soon after General Hood's courier passed us we began to hear the artillery ammunition exploding in Atlanta.   All was burned that could not be carried away on the march, as we now had no railroad transportation.   After burning the arms, ammunition, and stores that could not be transported, General Hood moved out with his army, and the Federals took undisputed possession of the city the next day.   General Hood, after burning his supplies, had moved out during the night eastwardly and by a circuitous march joined his other forces near Lovejoy Station. General Sherman soon abandoned Jonesboro, moved his army into and around Atlanta and two tired armies rested.   Sherman reported his loss in this campaign at 34,514, quite a large army in itself.

Our army settled down for the time being near Jonesboro, Ross' brigade doing outpost duty.   The ranks of the brigade had become very much depleted by the losses in killed, wounded, and captured during the Atlanta campaign, and the companies were temporarily consolidated.   This caused the regiments of the brigade, except the Third Texas, to have on hand a number of supernumerary company officers.   The Third having more officers in prisons and hospitals than the others, only had about enough officers after consolidation.   These officers, with consent of the commanders, agreed to organize themselves into a scouting party.   I had permission to join them, and as this offered some recreation, or at least a diversion,

I did so, being the only member from the Third. They were all gallant and experienced officers and jovial companionable fellows.

We organized by selecting Captain H. W. Wade of the Sixth Texas commander. I cannot now recall all of them, but among them were Captains O. P. Preston, Reuben Simpson, Cook, and Broughton, and Lieutenants W. J. Swain, Thompson Morris, W. W. McClathie, Bridges, and Park. We were joined by the gallant Captain Reams, of Missouri, whose command had surrendered at the fall of Vicksburg, and who, having gone to Missouri to recruit his command, was captured and imprisoned, but had escaped into Canada, and from there made his way back to General Hood's army. We were sent on duty in the country lying north of the West Point Railroad and south of the Chattahoochee River, west and northwest of Atlanta—this being a large scope of country not occupied by either army and liable to be depredated upon by the enemy. Campbellton, the county seat of Campbell County, was a town of some importance situated on the south bank of the Chattahoochee River, some thirty miles northwestwardly from Atlanta. The Federal outpost in this direction was twelve or fifteen miles out from the city.

Our duties were performed for several weeks without incident worthy of mention. We were sometimes in the territory over which we had fought during the summer, and a more desolate country I never saw; not a domestic animal or fowl, and scarcely a bird, could be seen; the woods, where we had fed our horses shelled corn, had grown up in green corn more than knee high, and there were no animals to crop

it down; the fences had all been torn down to build
barricades, and the crops had been without cultiva-
tion or protection since the early summer; the corn
had made small ears and the sorghum had grown up
into little trifling stalks, and the people who lived
hereabouts were subsisting on corn bread made of
grated meal and syrup made in the crudest manner.
Oh, the devastation and horrors of war! They must
be seen to be realized.

One morning we met Lieutenant Bob Lee, with his
scouts, and it was agreed that we would spend the
day together on a trip towards the river between
Campbellton and Sherman's outpost. Bob Lee was
a fine scout, a member of the Ninth Texas Cavalry
who had been promoted from the ranks to first lieutenant for his efficiency. Lee's scouts numbered
twenty, while we numbered twenty-one, all well
armed with Colt's revolvers and well mounted. On
our way we picked up Pem Jarvis, of Company K,
Third Texas, who was glad to join us. Pem had
the only gun in the company, and no pistol.

We moved north by any road or trail found to
lead to the right direction, until about noon, when
we struck the rear of a farm lying in a little valley.
Along the opposite ridge ran the " ridge road " from
Atlanta to Campbellton, probably half a mile distant. Near the road, in a strip of timber, stood a
farmhouse. Near the house we heard a gun fire and
a hog squeal. Throwing down the fence we rode in
and moved across cautiously, so as not to be seen
from the house. Passing out through a pair of
draw-bars, three or four of the men galloped up to
the house and into the yard, where they found two

Federal soldiers in the act of dressing a hog they had just killed. From them we learned that a party of about sixty cavalrymen, in charge of an officer, and having with them two four-mule wagons, had just passed, going in the direction of Campbellton. We started off, leaving the hog killers in charge of two of our men, and filed into the road. At the first house on the road, supposed to be Dr. Hornsby's, two ladies were in the act of mounting their horses at the gate. They were crying, and told us that some Yankee soldiers had passed there and insulted them, and that they were going to headquarters to ask for protection. They estimated the number at about sixty, with two wagons. This was about five miles from Campbellton.

We sent two of our scouts ahead to look for them, as there is also a road from Campbellton to Atlanta called the river road. If they returned by the ridge road we would meet them, if by the river road we would miss them. The scouts were to ascertain this matter and report. We moved on to within about two miles of the town and formed a line in the brush, a few steps south of the road and parallel with it, where, with bridles and pistols well in hand, we patiently waited the return of our scouts. The road from our position, towards town as far as we could see it, ran on a rough down grade and was lined with thick black jack brush. From here it was impossible for a horseman to get into the river road without going into town. The intention was, if they came our way, to wait until their column came up in our front and charge them in flank.

In due time we heard our scouts coming at a gallop, and looking up we saw they were being pursued by two Federals. One of the Federals reined up and stopped before he got in our front, while the other rode along nearly the entire front of our line, fired his gun at our scouts, ·cussed the d——d rebels, then stopped, and stood as if waiting for the column, which was then slowly moving up the hill. We could hear them driving milch cows, which they had taken from citizens, and accompanied by wagons loaded with the fruits of their day's robbery, such as tobacco, chickens, and turkeys. The fellow in our front furnished such a tempting target that one of our men fired, and the Federal dropped from his horse. This was sufficient to spoil the ambush, and we instantly spurred our horses into the road, gave a loud yell, and charged at full speed down the rough road, into the head of their column. As we approached them they seemed almost to forget the use of their seven-shooting rifles in an effort to reverse their column, and before they could accomplish this we were in among them, and they ran for dear life back to gain the river road. We went along with them to town, and they fired back at us vigorously, and powder burned some of our men in the face, but no one of our men received as much as a scratch. We were better armed for such a contest than they were, for though they had good rifles, their pistols were few, while we carried from two to four Colt's revolvers apiece.

Jarvis' horse became unmanageable in the excitement and ran under some black jack, and knocked Jarvis' gun out of his hand and plunged in among the enemy, passing by several of them while Jarvis had nothing to defend himself with. Some of them were in the act of shooting him in the back, but invariably Bob Lee or someone else would save him by shooting his assailant in the back of the head. The foremost and best mounted men, about twenty in number, with one wagon, got through the town. We followed them a few hundred yards and turned back. We had twelve prisoners unhurt, and going back over the road we found fourteen dead and fifteen wounded. We had in our possession one wagon and team, thirty or forty rifles, a few pistols, and a number of horses with their rigging.

As I was going back on the road I came to an elderly wounded man just outside of the road. I reined up my horse, and as I did so he reached out a trembling hand, in which he held a greasy leather pocketbook, and said: " Here, take this, but please don't kill me." I told him to put up his pocketbook; that I would neither take that nor his life; that I only wanted his arms.

The slightly wounded men, who would likely be able to fight again very soon, we put into the wagon, and mounting the unhurt ones on the captured horses we paired off with them, and thus started for our own lines. I rode with one of the prisoners, who was quite a talkative fellow. Upon asking him why it was that so many of their men refused to surrender, and allowed themselves to be shot, he said: " Our officers have told us that Ross's brigade never shows prisoners any quarter, but will rob and murder them; and we knew it was Ross's brigade as soon as you yelled that way." I told him that was a great slander on the brigade; that no men would treat prisoners more kindly; that sometimes we were hard up for clothes and would take an overcoat, or blanket, or something of the kind from a fellow that was well supplied. " Oh," said he, " that's nothing; *we* do that." I then said to him: " I believe your boots will fit me, and these brogans of mine will do you just as well at Andersonville." He said, " All right," and instantly he dismounted and pulled his boots off. We traded, and I had a good pair of kip boots that fit me, and he had brogan shoes, and was apparently happy. He asked me how it was that we were so much better mounted than they were. I explained that we furnished our own horses, and we must keep them or go to the infantry, and that made our men good horsemasters; while the United States Government furnished them with horses and they knew that when they rode one to death they would get another.

We continued our scouting duties in the same section of country until the early days of October, when General Hood moved around in General Sherman's rear, and began destroying his communications, capturing supplies and provisions. Sherman moved out of Atlanta and followed Hood until the latter came to the vicinity of Rome. General Hood unwilling to risk a battle in the open field, crossed the Coosa River, moving by way of Gadsden, Ala., towards Guntersville on the Tennessee River. When General Sherman discovered this movement he turned back towards Atlanta, devastating the country and despoiling the citizens as he went.

With General Hood's movement across the Coosa River he began his last campaign, and the last cam-

paign for the Army of the Tennessee. His intention was to cross the Tennessee at Guntersville and
march on Nashville, but he changed his mind and
moved down the river to near Decatur, Tuscumbia,
and Florence, Ross's brigade being in front of
Decatur, then occupied by the Federals. General
Sherman returning to Atlanta, that city was burned,
and leaving the smoking ruins behind him, he entered
upon his grand march to the sea, with none of General Hood's army, save General Wheeler's cavalry,
to molest him in his work of devastation.

A day or two after we got to Decatur General
Ross ordered our scouting party back up the river
to ascertain, if we could, what the enemy was doing
in the rear of that place. We moved up on the south
side of the river and stopped between Triana and
Whitesburg. These towns were garrisoned and the
river patrolled by gunboats. We remained in this
neighborhood without any further instructions for
some weeks. Here I found my half-brother, J. J.
Ashworth, who lived on the south bank of the river
about fifteen miles from Huntsville, and about three
miles above Triana. In this neighborhood were a
number of my acquaintances from Madison County,
refugeeing, as Huntsville, Brownsboro, and other
towns were also garrisoned by the enemy. Several
of us crossed the river afoot and remained some days
in Madison County. But for the negroes we could
have had a pleasant time, as every negro in the
country was a spy who would run to report anything
that looked suspicious to them, to one of the near-by
garrisons, so we dared not allow them to see us. I
knew the white people, and knew that they were loyal

to our cause, but they could not allow their own negroes to know that they did anything for us, so that we, and they, too, had to be exceedingly careful.

In crossing the river we had to watch for gunboats, make the passage during the night in a canoe, which must be drawn out and hidden, else the first passing gunboat would destroy it. Some three miles north of the river, in the bottom, lived Alexander Penland, a Presbyterian minister, a true and loyal friend to the Confederacy, and three or four miles further on, towards Huntsville, lived William Lanier, Burwell Lanier and William Matkins, the two latter on the Huntsville and Triana road. Dr. William Leftwich also lived in the same neighborhood. All were good, trustworthy men, whom I knew well. Since some of them had taken the non-combatant's oath they were allowed to go in and out of town at will, and from them I could learn of any movements along the M. & C. Railroad. We crossed the river after night, and being in possession of Mr. Penland's countersign, we found our way to his house, late at night, after the household was all asleep. I went to a certain front window, tapped lightly and whistled like a partridge. Soon Mr. Penland thrust his head out and in a whisper inquired who we were and what was wanted. I explained to him briefly, and retired to a brush thicket near by, where early next morning he brought us cooked provisions. In order to do this he had to get up and cook for us himself before any of his negroes were awake. The next night we slept in William Lanier's farm and were fed by him in the same way. We crossed the Triana road and went to the top of a small mountain, from which we could see Huntsville. A rainy season set in and we found shelter in Burwell Lanier's gin-house, where he fed us. When we thought of recrossing the Tennessee we found that Indian Creek, which we had to cross, was outrageously high, spreading away out over the bottom. We spent a good part of an afternoon in constructing a raft by tying logs together with vines to enable us to cross that night. Just east of William Lanier's farm there was a large negro quarter, where idle and vicious negroes were in the habit of congregating, and inasmuch as their system of espionage upon the white people of the neighborhood was very annoying, upon the suggestion of some of our friends we determined to raid this place before we left, carry off some of these meddlesome blacks and send them to some government works in south Alabama.

Accordingly after dark we visited the quarter under the guise of recruiting officers from Whitesburg, told them we had been fighting for their freedom for about three years, and the time had now come for them to help us, and we had come for every able-bodied man to go with us to Whitesburg and join the army. I had our men call me Brown, for fear some of them might know me. It was laughable to hear the various excuses rendered for not going into the service. A lot of Confederate conscripts could not have thought up more physical ailments. We finally gathered up six that we decided were able for service, promising they should have a medical examination, and if they were really unfit for service they would be excused. Among them was a powerful, large, muscular black fellow that belonged to Jink Jordan. He had joined the army and, tiring of his job, was now a deserter, and we could see that he was greatly scared and very much opposed to going with us.

Upon leaving the negro houses we went through the field and the woods directly to our raft on the creek and had a great time getting across. The clouds were thick, it was intensely dark, and our means of crossing very poor. We had to make a number of trips, as we could only float three or four men, including the two that used the poles, at one time. In the confusion and darkness two of the prisoners had escaped, and two had just crossed, including the big deserter, when it became my duty to guard them with a short Enfield rifle belonging to one of the men. Having their hands tied with a cord and then tied together back to back, I was not uneasy about keeping them, but before I realized what they were doing they had slipped their hands through the cord and were running through the brush. When the big deserter had gone some twelve or fifteen steps I shot him. He fell at the fire of the gun, but before I could get to him he scrambled up and went crashing through the brush like a stampeding ox. I learned afterwards that he went into Huntsville to a hospital for treatment, and that the ball had gone through the muscle of his arm and plowed into his breast, but not deep enough to be fatal. We finally reached the bank of the river about one or two o'clock in the morning, with two of our prisoners. We then had to hoot like an owl until some one on the other side should wake up, and, hearing the signal, would bring us a canoe, which was finally done, and we crossed over in safety.

We crossed the river several times during our stay in the neighborhood, particularly one very cold night, when several of us passed over, at the request of Mr. Penland, to transfer his pork to the south side. He had killed a lot of hogs, and was afraid the meat might be taken from him, or that he would be ordered out of the Federal lines as others had been, and he wished to place it in the hands of a friend south of the river for safety. We managed to get an old rickety canoe opposite his place, and crossed early in the night, and again played the rôle of Federal soldiers, as no one on his place but himself must know our real mission. Mrs. Penland had known me from childhood, but as she had lost her mind I did not fear recognition, and while Nancy, their negro woman, also had known me, she failed to recognize me, as I was Mr. Brown of the Federal army. We marched up and called for the man of the house, and when Mr. Penland came forward we told him we were rather short of rations down in Triana, and were out looking for meat, and wished to know if he had any. He acknowledged that he had just killed some meat, but only enough for his family use, and had none to spare. We were bound to have meat, and agreed to leave him one hog, and then yoked up a pair of oxen and hitched them to a wagon. While we were in the smokehouse preparing to take the meat out, Mr. Penland's two little girls, about nine and eleven, came crying around us, and in a most pitiful manner begged us not to take all of papa's meat; and poor Mrs. Penland came to the door and said: "Men, please don't take my little boy's pony." When we had hauled all the meat to the river bank and returned the wagon, it was nearly midnight, and we compelled the woman Nancy to get up and prepare us a warm supper. After supper we returned to the river and floated the hogs across in our old canoe.

At this time my brother's son, George Ashworth, a gallant boy about sixteen years old, who had taken his father's place in General Roddy's command, was at home on furlough. One day a thief, believed to be a straggler from General Wheeler's command, took his horse from a lot some distance from the house, and carried him off. Lieutenant McClatchie and myself mounted a pony and a mule of my brother's and attempted to overtake him. We followed him as far as Atlanta, but failed to catch him, and then went into the city and viewed the wreck that Sherman had left behind him: thirty-six hundred houses were in ruins, including the best part of the city. This was Saturday, and being tired we went down to the neighborhood of Jonesboro and remained with some of McClatchie's acquaintances until Monday morning. We were hospitably entertained at the home of Colonel Tidwell, and enjoyed a quiet rest in the company of Miss Mattie Tidwell and Miss Eva Camp.

One evening we passed through the town of Cave Springs, a locality with which I had become familiar while we were campaigning here. On the road we were to travel, at the first house after leaving town, two or three miles out, there lived a tall dignified old gentleman and his handsome young married daughter whose husband was in the army. They lived in a large two-story house, and a large commodious barn, with all other necessary out houses for comfort and convenience, had stood on his premises when I was there before—the barn filled to overflowing with wheat, oats, and corn. Just across the road in front of the house, and stretching across the valley, was his large productive farm, covered with a heavy crop of ungathered corn. While this was the condition, I had come to this house at night, traveling in the same direction, and talked myself almost hoarse without being able to procure from this old gentleman a single ear of corn for my horse or a morsel of food for myself, although he knew I must go eight miles to the next house on the road. I didn't ask, nor did I wish, to enter his house, but only wanted a feed of corn and a little bread and meat. As we approached the house McClatchie proposed halting, to stay all night—provided we could. I related my earlier experience, but we stopped nevertheless.

Upon seeing us halt, the old gentleman came stepping down to the gate and spoke very kindly, and we asked him if we could spend the night with him. He said such accommodations as he could offer us we would be welcome to, adding: " I have no stables for your horses. Sherman's army passed this way and burned my barn, with its contents, my stables, and in fact carried off or destroyed everything I had to eat or feed on, and left me and my daughter without a mouthful of anything to eat. They carried every hog, every fowl, and every pound of meat, and even rolled my syrup out of the cellar, knocked the heads out of the barrels and poured the syrup out on the ground, but I will do the best I can for you." His daughter, too, was very hospitable. At the supper table she detailed all the horrors of Sherman's visit, and the distressful condition they were left in, how they had to go to a neighbor's to borrow a few ears of corn to grate them for bread, and concluded by saying: " But as long as I have a piece of bread I will divide it with a Confederate soldier." After supper she invited us into the parlor, where she had a nice piano and treated us to music. Verily " our friends, the enemy," had converted one family!

CHAPTER XVII

MY LAST BATTLE

Tories and Deserters—A Tragic Story—A Brutal Murder
—The Son's Vow—Vengeance—A Southern Heroine—Seeking
Our Command—Huntsville—A Strange Meeting—We Find the
Division—The Battle in the Fog—My Last Battle.

HADEN PRYOR, who lived eight miles west on the same road, was a whole-souled, big-hearted old gentleman, who also had a large place and plenty of everything to live on, and whose hospitality towards a Confederate soldier was unbounded. His boys were in the army in Virginia, and he and his wife were at home alone. I had stayed with him while hunting a blacksmith shop, and found that a tired Confederate soldier was more than welcome to his home. Lonely, and impatient for the war to close, that his gallant boys might come home, he would sit out on his front veranda and play solitaire, and was glad to see a soldier come, and sorry to see him leave. He had a nephew in our regiment that I knew and liked, and I had fallen in love with this old gentleman. Next morning McClatchie and I, when we came to his house, called to pay him our respects and to tell him good-by.

This neighborhood, or rather the neighborhood just south of this, and a considerable scope of country lying along the western border of Georgia and the eastern border of Alabama, was infested with a class of the meanest white men on earth—Tories and deserters, men too cowardly to fight in either army, but mean and unscrupulous enough to do anything. We knew they were there, but while our army·was in the neighborhood they were never seen.   Since the armies had left they were growing bolder, and we were told at Mr. Pryor's that morning about some of their thievery and robbery.   Providence protected us that day.   Here were two roads, one to the left and one to the right, and we could follow one or the other and reach our destination in the same number of miles.   The matter was left to me, and, without thinking of danger, I selected the right-hand road. On that day the left-hand road was waylaid by a band of these infamous characters and every Confederate soldier who attempted to pass the road was robbed of horse, arms, and everything of any value, and one or two of them murdered.   These soldiers had been left behind slightly wounded or sick, and were on their way to overtake their commands.   One of the murdered ones belonged to Ross's brigade.

Since the war I have heard, from a reliable source, a tragic story of this Pryor family, which, if told in detail, would sound like fiction.   It seems that in the spring of 1865 a band of these cut-throats, eight in number, rode up to Haden Pryor's gate and without provocation shot him while he was standing in his front yard in presence of his wife; as he turned and was in the act of returning to his house he fell in his front veranda, a corpse.   This was a few days after General Lee's surrender.   His oldest son, John, and a younger one, with eight or ten other Confederates, on their way home that night came within eight or ten miles of their homes, when, tired and footsore, they lay down to rest until morning.

John Pryor, haunted by a strange presentiment, could not sleep, and determined he would quietly leave the camp and go on to his father's house. While he was dressing one of the others woke and said: "Hello, John, what are you up to?" "I am going home," said John. "Wait a minute," said the other, "and I'll go too." From that one by one they all roused up and were soon on the road again. Arriving at home, John Pryor found his father a bloody corpse and his mother a widow. His mother told him how it all happened, and gave him the names of his father's murderers. The next day the funeral took place, and the noble father who had so patiently waited and longed for the return of his soldier boys was laid under the sod.

Over his father's grave John Pryor made a vow that he would not engage in any business whatever as long as one of his father's murderers was alive, and starting out upon his fixed purpose he killed one or two of them before the gang became alarmed. The rest now became panic-stricken and fled the country, hiding in different States. John hunted them constantly and relentlessly for weeks and months, until the weeks grew into years, and as he found them they were sent to their final account, one by one, until finally he found the last and least guilty one in Travis County, Texas, a few miles from Austin. It was in the spring of the year, and the man was plowing when John walked into the field where he was. Seeing John coming and recognizing him, he stopped his horse and, waiting until he was within a few steps of him, he said, " John, I know what you have come for; but I will ask you to let me go to the house and tell my wife and children good-by." John consented, and they went to the house, where were the innocent wife and two small children in a comfortable little home. The husband and father then said: " John, I never hurt your father; I didn't want those fellows to kill him, and told them not to do it." " I remember that my mother told me something about this," replied John, " and said you were the only one who said a word against the murder of my father; and now I will retract my vow as to you, and leave you with your wife and children."

Now feeling that he had fulfilled his mission, Pryor returned to his home, and devoting his attention to business became a prosperous and successful man.

As we continued our way back to north Alabama, crossing Black Creek, we came to the residence of Mrs. Sansom. Here we stopped under pretense of lighting our pipes, and remained for an hour, merely to get a look at the young heroine, Miss Emily Sansom, the young girl who rode behind General Forrest and piloted him to a ford on the creek where he was in hot pursuit of Colonel Straight and his men. This story of Emily Sansom's heroism has been published so often that most people are familiar with it. She now lives, a widow, in Upshur County, Texas.*

* Since the above was written, this Southern heroine has passed to that bourne from which no traveler returns.

We pushed on to our former headquarters on the Tennessee River, to find that our people had been gone ever so long. General Hood had crossed the river about the last of November, Decatur, Huntsville, Triana, and Whitesburg had all been evacuated by the enemy, and our army was in middle Tennessee. Our scouts, as we afterwards learned, had crossed the river, passed through Huntsville and moved up to the vicinity of Shelbyville. Our command had participated in the fighting on the advance into Tennessee, had been in the battle of Franklin, and was then sent to Murfreesboro.

McClatchie and myself crossed the river and spent the night at the home of our friend, Rev. Alexander Penland. Next day we went into Huntsville, and while waiting for our horses to be shod I had time to see a number of my friends, among them Miss Aggie Scott, from whom I learned that my old friend, W. H. Powers, and his wife, were sojourning in New London, Conn. We went out in the evening and spent the night at the home of Mr. William Matkin, a few miles down the Triana road. Late at night Rev. Lieutenant-Colonel William D. Chadick came to Mr. Matkin's, afoot, tired and somewhat excited, and informed us that a division of Federal cavalry had entered Huntsville that afternoon. He had been at home with his family, and told an interesting story of his escape. He had left his home, gone across lots, and reaching the Female seminary lot, had hidden under the floor of the seminary until nightfall, when he had made his way through back lots and fields until he was well out of town. He then found his way around to the Triana road and here he was.

General McCook was in command of the forces that had come in so unexpectedly, and learning that Colonel Chadick was at home, showed great anxiety to capture him, so much so that he visited his home in person. Finding Mrs. Chadick there, he interrogated her as to the whereabouts of her husband. She told him that Colonel Chadick was not at home. He seemed incredulous, and cross-questioned her closely, when something in her tone or her favor led him to change the conversation, and he said to her: "Madam, where are you from?" She answered, "I am from Steubenville, Ohio." "I am also from Steubenville, Ohio. What was your maiden name?" She answered, "My maiden name was Cook." "Were you Miss Jane Cook?" said he. She answered, "I was." Then said he: "Do you remember, many years ago, one Sunday morning, when you were on your way to Sunday school, that some little boys were cutting up in the street near the Episcopal church and a policeman was about to take them up when you interceded in their behalf and he let them off?" She answered, "I do." "I was one of those boys," said he, "and now, madam, I am ready to do anything in my power for your protection and comfort." Guards were placed at her gates, and not a soldier allowed to enter the premises while General McCook's command remained there.

Colonel Chadick was well known to me, he having been pastor of the Cumberland Presbyterian church in Huntsville for several years while I lived there. He first entered the army as chaplain of the Fourth Alabama Infantry, and was with that famous regiment in the first battle of Manassas. He was after-

LIEUTENANT S. B. BARRON
Third Texas Cavalry
Photo 1882

wards made major of an Alabama battalion, of which
Nick Davis was lieutenant-colonel, later consolidated
with Coltart's battalion, to become the Fiftieth Alabama Infantry, when John G. Coltart became colonel
and William D. Chadick lieutenant-colonel. At this
time he had an idea of raising a new regiment of
cavalry, and wished me to return and raise a company for the regiment or else take a position on
his staff, but we were now too near the end.

McClatchie and myself started out next morning
and went up the Huntsville road a short distance,
when we came in sight of a small party of Federal
cavalry in the act of turning back. We took a road
that led us into the Athens road at John N. Drake's
place, where we learned that another party had come
out there, and turned back. We then made our way
directly to Pulaski, Tenn., on towards Columbia, and
found the division on the Columbia pike hotly engaged with the enemy, who was pushing General
Hood's retreat. Our rear-guard was commanded by
General Forrest, and consisted of his own cavalry,
Jackson's cavalry division, and about fifteen hundred infantry, under Major-General Walthal. The
infantry were trans-Mississippi troops, including
Ector's and Granberry's brigades. General Hood's
main army was retreating by different roads towards
Bainbridge, where we were to cross the Tennessee
River. Jackson's division of cavalry and the infan-
try of the rear-guard were on the main road, while
General Forrest's cavalry was protecting other
roads. We were uncomfortably crowded on the turnpike, but we left it at Pulaski, crossed Richland
Creek on a bridge, and fired the bridge. The Fed-

erals soon came up and extinguished the fire, however, and then came pouring across the bridge, but as it was now late in the afternoon they did not attack any more for the day.

The next morning General Forrest selected a favorable position in the hills a few miles below Pulaski, masked his batteries, and formed his infantry in ambush, and, when the enemy came on us, attacked them with artillery, infantry, and cavalry, and after a sharp little battle drove them back handsomely, with some loss, capturing one piece of artillery and taught them that in the hills it was imprudent to rush upon an enemy recklessly. For the remainder of that day we were permitted to move quietly down the road unmolested.

That night one of General Frank Armstrong's Mississippi cavalry regiments was left on picket, and we moved on a mile or two and camped by the roadside. Just after daylight the next morning our Mississippi regiments came clattering in, closely pursued by the enemy's cavalry. We hastily formed a line across the road and checked the enemy, and then moved on to Sugar Creek and formed another ambush. There was a dense fog along the creek, such as I never saw in the interior. Our infantry were formed along the creek bank just above the crossing, and the cavalry in column of fours in the road forty or fifty yards back from the ford of the creek, and thus, in the fog, we were as completely concealed as if midnight darkness had prevailed. The infantry remained perfectly quiet until the head of the enemy's column was in the act of crossing the creek, when suddenly, with a yell they plunged through the creek and charged them. This threw the head of their column into confusion, when our cavalry charged them in column at a gallop, and pressed them back two or three miles. *And this was the last fight I was ever in!*

CHAPTER XVIII

ROSS' REPORT OF BRIGADE'S LAST CAMPAIGN

Ross' Report—Repulse a Reconnoitering Party—Effective Fighting Strength—Advance Guard—The Battle at Campbellsville—Results—Thompson's Station—Harpeth River—Murfreesboro—Lynville—Pulaski—Sugar Creek—Losses During Campaign—Captures—Acknowledgments.

HEADQUARTERS ROSS' BRIGADE, J. C. D.
CORINTH, MISS., Jan. 12, 1865.

CAPTAIN:

I have the honor to submit the following report of the part performed by my brigade in the late campaign into Middle Tennessee.

First, however, and by way of introduction, it is proper to premise that we bore a full share in the arduous duties required of the cavalry in the Georgia campaign, and were particularly active during the operations of the army upon the enemy's line of communication.

October 24, in compliance with orders from division commander, I withdrew from my position near Cave Springs, Ga., crossed the Coosa River at Gadsden the day following, and by rapid marches arrived in front of Decatur, Ala., on the evening of the 29th. Was here halted to observe the movements of the enemy while the army rested at Tuscumbia. On the morning of November 8 a strong reconnoitering party, consisting of three regiments of infantry and one of cavalry, coming out from Decatur on the Courtland road, was promptly met, and after a sharp skirmish driven back with some loss. The next day, being relieved by a portion of General Roddy's command, we retired down the valley to Town Creek and rested until the 18th, when we were ordered across the river at Florence, and moving at once to the front of the army, took position with the other cavalry commands on Shoal Creek.

November 21, all things being ready for the advance, we were ordered forward, following in the rear of Armstrong's Brigade. The effective fighting strength of my command at this time was as follows: Third Regiment Texas Cavalry, 218; Sixth Regiment Texas Cavalry, 218; Ninth Regiment Texas Cavalry, 110; Twenty-seventh Regiment Texas Cavalry, 140; making a total of 686. With this small force we joined the advance into Tennessee, strong in heart and resolved to make up in zeal and courage what was wanting in numbers. The day after crossing Shoal Creek, General Armstrong, having still the advance, came up with Federal cavalry at Lawrenceburg. The fighting was chiefly with artillery, Captain Young's battery being freely used, and to good effect. About sunset the enemy withdrew in the direction of Pulaski. Early the next morning I was ordered to take the advance and move out on the Pulaski road. About twelve miles from Lawrenceburg we came upon the Federal pickets and drove them in. The Third Texas now dismounted and with two squadrons from the Twenty-seventh Texas moved forward and attacked the enemy, forcing him from his successive positions and following him up so vigorously as to compel the precipitate abandonment of his camps and all his forage. The next day, having still the advance, when within five miles of Pulaski, we changed direction to the left, following the route taken by the enemy in his retreat the evening before, and arriving about noon in sight of the little village, Campbellsville, I found a large force of cavalry, which proved to be Hatch's division, drawn up to resist us. Lieutenant-Colonel Boggess was ordered promptly to dismount his regiment, the Third Texas, and move it to the front. Young's battery was hurried up from the rear, placed in position and, supported by the Sixth Texas (Colonel Jack Wharton, commanding), commenced shelling the enemy's lines. In the meanwhile the Ninth Texas and the Legion were drawn up in column, in the field to the right of the wood, to be used as circumstances might require. These dispositions completed, I watched with interest the effect of the shelling from our battery, and very soon discovered from the movements of the enemy, an intention to withdraw, whereupon, believing this to be the proper movement, I ordered everything forward. The Ninth Texas and Legion, led by their respective commanders, Colonel Jones and Lieutenant-Colonel Whitfield, rushed forward at a gallop, and passing through the village, fell upon the enemy's moving squadrons with such irresistible force as to scatter them in every direction, pursuing and capturing numbers of prisoners, horses, equipment, small arms, accouterments, and four (4) stands of colors. The enemy made no effort to regain the field from which he had been driven, but while endeavoring to with-

draw his broken and discomfited squadrons was attacked vigorously in flank by a portion of General
Armstrong's brigade, and his rout made complete.
The last of his forces, in full flight, disappeared in
the direction of Lynville about sunset, and we saw
no more of them south of Duck River. Our loss
in the fight at Campbellsville was only five (5) men
wounded, while our captures (I found upon investigation) summed up to be eighty-four (84) prisoners,
and all their horses, equipments, and small arms, four
(4) stands of colors and sixty-five (65) beef cattle.
Without further opposition we arrived the next day
in front of Columbia, and took the position assigned
us on the Chapel Hill pike.

November 26, we remained in front of the enemy's
works, skirmishing freely and keeping up a lively
demonstration. On the morning of the 27th, being
relieved by the infantry, we were ordered over to
Shelbyville pike, and camped the following night
on Fountain Creek. Crossing Duck River the next
morning, at the mill, nine miles above Columbia, we
were directed thence to the right (on the Shelbyville road), and when near the Lewisburg and Franklin pike, again encountered the Federal cavalry. A
spirited engagement ensued, begun by the Third
Texas, which being detached to attack a train of
wagons moving in the direction of Franklin, succeeded in reaching the pike, but was there met by a
superior force of Yankees and driven back. Seeing
this, I had Colonel Hawkins to hurry his regiment
(the Legion) to the assistance of the Third, and ordered a charge, which was made in gallant style, and
resulted in forcing the Yankees from the field in con-

fusion, and with the loss of several prisoners and the colors of the Seventh Ohio Cavalry. In the meanwhile Colonel Wharton, with the Sixth Texas, charged into the pike to the right of where the Third and Legion were engaged, capturing an entire company of the Seventh Ohio Cavalry, three (3) stands of colors, several wagons loaded with ordnances, and a considerable number of horses, with their equipments. The Ninth Texas (Colonel Jones), having been detached early in the evening to guard the road leading to our right, with the exception of a slight skirmish with the enemy's pickets, in which several prisoners were taken, was not otherwise engaged during the evening. It was now after night and very dark. The enemy had disappeared from our front in direction of Franklin, but before establishing camps it was thought prudent to ascertain if any force had been cut off and yet remained between us and the river. Colonel Hawkins was therefore ordered up the pike with his regiment to reconnoiter, and had proceeded but a short distance before he was met by a brigade of Federal cavalry. An exciting fight ensued, lasting about half an hour, when the enemy, having much the larger force, succeeded in passing by us, receiving as he did so a severe fire into his flanks. This ceased the operations for the day, and we were allowed to bivouac, well pleased with the prospect of rest, after so much fatiguing exercise.

At Hunts cross roads the next day, when the other commands of cavalry took the left and moved upon Spring Hill, my brigade was advanced upon the road to Franklin. Afterwards, in obedience to

orders of the division commander, we turned towards Thompson's Station, being now in rear of
the Federal army, which still held its position on
Rutherford's Creek. The Yankee cavalry, completely whipped, had disappeared in the direction
of Franklin, and did not again show itself that day.
When near Thompson's Station I discovered a few
wagons moving on the pike, and sent Colonel Jones,
with the Ninth and Legion, to intercept and capture them. At the same time the Sixth and Third
Texas were drawn up in line, and a squadron from
the latter dispatched to destroy the depot. Colonel
Jones was partially successful, capturing and destroying one wagon and securing the team. He then
charged a train of cars which came up from the
direction of Franklin, when the engineer becoming
frightened, cut the engine loose and ran off southward. The train, thus freed, began to retrograde,
and in spite of the obstructions thrown in its way
and the efforts of the men to stop it, rolled back under the guns of a blockhouse and was saved. The
guard, however, and all the men on the train were
forced to jump off, and became our prisoners. I
now had the railroad bridge destroyed, in consequence of which the engine that escaped from us,
and another, became the prizes of our army the
next day. In the meantime the enemy at the depot,
observing the approach of the squadron from the
Third Texas, set fire to all of his valuables, including
a train of cars loaded with ordnance, and evacuated
the place. Having accomplished all that could be
effected in the station, we withdrew late in the evening, dropping back to the left of Spring Hill and

halted until I could communicate with the division
commander. About midnight I received the order
directing me to again " Strike the pike " and attack
the enemy's train, then in full retreat to Franklin; moved out at once to obey the order, guided
by an officer of General Forrest's staff who knew
the country. When within half a mile of the pike
I dismounted three (3) of my regiments, leaving
the Ninth Texas mounted to guard their horses,
and cautiously advancing on foot, got within one
hundred yards of the enemy's train without being
discovered. The Legion (Colonel Hawkins commanding) having the advance, fronted into line, fired a
well-directed volley, killing several Yankees and
mules, and rushed forward with a yell, producing
among the teamsters and wagon guards a perfect
stampede.   The Yankees lost thirty-nine (39)
wagons, some of which were destroyed, and others
abandoned for the want of the teams, which we
brought off. Remaining in possession of the pike
for half an hour, we withdrew upon the approach
of several bodies of infantry, which coming up in
opposite directions, by mistake got to shooting into
each other, and fired several volleys before finding
out their error. Having remounted our horses, we
remained on the hill overlooking the pike until
daylight, and saw the Yankee army in full retreat.
While this was passing a regiment of cavalry appearing in the open field in our front was charged
by the Sixth Texas, completely routed and driven
to his infantry column. Soon after this we again
pushed forward, keeping parallel with the pike,
upon which our infantry was moving, crossed Har-

peth River in the evening, about three miles above Franklin, only a small force of the enemy appearing to dispute the passage. Half a mile from the river we came upon a regiment of Yankee cavalry drawn up in line. This the Ninth Texas at once charged and routed, but was met by a larger force, and in turn compelled to give back, the enemy following in close pursuit. The Third Texas now rushed forward, checked the advancing squadrons of the Yankees, and then hurled them back, broken and disorganized, capturing several prisoners and driving the others back upon their heavier lines. The gallant bearing of the men and officers of the Third and Ninth Texas on this occasion is deserving of special commendation, and it affords me much gratification to record to the honor of these noble regiments that charges made by them at Harpeth River have never been, and cannot be, surpassed by cavalry of any nation. By the charge of the Third Texas we gained possession of an eminence overlooking the enemy's position and held it until late in the evening, when discovering an intention on the part of the Yankee commander to advance his entire force, and being without any support, I withdrew to the south side of the river again. Very soon the enemy advanced his whole line, but finding we had recrossed the river again, retreated, and during the night withdrew from our front. The next day we moved forward, arrived in front of Nashville December 3, and took position on the Nolensville pike three miles from the city. Just in our front was a line of works, and wishing to ascertain what force occupied them, I had two squadrons of the Sixth Texas to dismount, deploy as skirmishers, and advance. We found the works held only by the enemy's skirmishers, who withdrew upon our approach. After this, being relieved by our infantry, we returned to the rear with orders to cook up rations. On the morning of December 5 the brigade was ordered to Lavergne; found there a small force of infantry, which took refuge inside the fort, and after slight resistance surrendered upon demand of the division commander. Moving thence to Murfreesboro, where within a few miles of the city the enemy's pickets were encountered, and after a stubborn resistance driven back by the Sixth and Third Texas, dismounted. A few days after this Major-General Forrest invested Murfreesboro with his cavalry and one (1) division of infantry. The duty assigned my brigade being to guard all the approaches to the city, from the Salem to the Woodbury pike inclusive, was very severe for so small a force, and almost every day there was heavy skirmishing on some portion of our line.

December 15, a train of cars from Stevenson, heavily laden with supplies for the garrison at Murfreesboro, was attacked about seven miles south of the city, and although guarded by a regiment of infantry, two hundred strong, was captured and burned. The train was loaded with sugar, coffee, hard bread, and bacon, and carried full two hundred thousand rations. The men guarding it fought desperately for about an hour, having a strong position in a cut of the railroad, but were finally routed by a most gallant charge of the Sixth Texas, supported by the Third Texas, and 150 of them captured.

The others escaped to blockhouses near by. The next day, in consequence of the reverses to our arms at Nashville, we were withdrawn from the front of Murfreesboro, ordered across to Triana, and thence to Columbia, crossing Duck River in the evening of the 18th.

December 24, while being in the rear of our army, the enemy charged my rear-guard at Lynville, with a heavy force, and threatened to break over all opposition, when the Sixth Texas hastily forming, met and hurled them back, administering a most wholesome check to their ardor. At the moment this occurred our columns were all in motion, and it was of the utmost importance to break the charge of the enemy on our rear. Too much credit, therefore, cannot be given the Sixth Texas, for gallant bearing on this occasion. Had it failed to check the enemy, my brigade, and probably the entire division, taken at disadvantage, might have suffered severely. At Richland Creek, when the cavalry took position later in the day, I was assigned a position on the right of the railroad, and in front of the creek. Soon afterwards, however, the enemy moving as if to cross above the bridge, I was withdrawn to the south side of the creek and took position on the hill near the railroad, skirmishing with the enemy in my front, holding him in check until our forces had all crossed the creek. We were then ordered to withdraw, and passing through Pulaski, again crossed Richland Creek and camped near Mr. Carter's for the night. The next day my brigade, alternating with General Armstrong in bringing up the rear,

had frequent skirmishes with the enemy's advance.
Nine miles from Pulaski, when the infantry halted
and formed, I was ordered on the right. Soon
after this the enemy made a strong effort to turn
our right flank, but failed, and was driven back.
About the same time the infantry charged and
captured his artillery, administering such an effec-
tual check that he did not again show himself that
day.

This done, we retired leisurely, and after night
bivouacked on Sugar Creek. Early the following
morning the Yankees, still not satisfied, made their
appearance, and our infantry again made dispositions to receive them. Reynolds' and Ector's brigades took position, and immediately in their rear
I had the Legion and Ninth Texas drawn up in
column of fours to charge, if an opportunity should
occur. The fog was very dense and the enemy therefore approached very cautiously. When near enough
to be seen, the infantry fired a volley and charged.
At the same time the Legion and Ninth Texas were
ordered forward, and passing through our infantry,
crossed the creek in the face of a terrible fire, over-
threw all opposition on the further side, and pursued the thoroughly routed foe near a mile, capturing twelve (12) prisoners and as many horses, besides killing numbers of others. The force opposed
to us here was completely whipped,—proved from
the statements of the prisoners to be Hammond's
brigade of cavalry. After this the Yankees did not
again show themselves, and without further inter-
ruption we recrossed the Tennessee River at Bainbridge on the evening of the 27th of December.

Our entire loss during the campaign sums up as follows:

COMMAND	KILLED		WOUNDED		CAPTURED		AGGREGATE
	OFFICERS	EN. MEN	OFFICERS	EN. MEN	OFFICERS	EN. MEN	
Third Texas Cavalry.		2	3	22	1	2	30
Sixth Texas Cavalry.		6	3	19		1	29
Ninth Texas Cavalry.		4		17		1	22
Texas Legion.......				6			6
Total.........		12	6	64	1	4	87

We captured on the trip and brought off five hun-dred and fifty (550) prisoners, as shown by the records of my provost-marshal, nine (9) stands of colors, several hundred horses and their equipments, and overcoats and blankets sufficient to supply my command. We destroyed, besides, two trains of cars, loaded, one with ordnance, and the other with com-missary stores; forty or fifty wagons and mules; and much other valuable property belonging to the Federal army. My brigade returned from Ten-nessee with horses very much jaded, but otherwise in no worse condition than when it started, its morale not in the least affected nor impaired by the evident demoralization which prevailed to a consid-erable extent throughout the larger portion of the army.

Before closing my report I desire to record an acknowledgment of grateful obligations to the gallant officers and brave men whom I have the honor to command. Entering upon the campaign poorly clad and illy prepared for undergoing its hardships, these worthy votaries of freedom nevertheless bore themselves bravely, and I did not hear a murmur, nor witness the least reluctance in the discharge of duty, however unpleasant. All did well, and to this I attribute in a great measure the unparalleled success which attended all our efforts during the campaign.

To Colonel D. W. Jones, Colonel E. R. Hawkins, Colonel Jack Wharton, Lieutenant-Colonel J. S. Boggess, who commanded their respective regiments; and Lieutenant-Colonel P. F. Ross and Major S. B. Wilson, Sixth Texas; Lieutenant-Colonel J. T. Whitfield and Major B. H. Nosworthy, of Legion; Major A. B. Stone, Third Texas; and Major H. C. Dial, Ninth Texas; also Captains Gurly, Plummer, Killough and Preston; Lieutenants Alexander and Sykes; members of my staff: I feel especially indebted for earnest, zealous, and efficient co-operation. These officers upon many trying occasions acquitted themselves with honor, and it affords me pleasure to be able to commend to the favorable notice of the Brigadier-General commanding.

I have the honor to be, Captain, very resp't,
Your obedient Servant,

Official: L. S. Ross,
A. A. G. " 59 "   *Brig. Gen'l., J. C.*

CHAPTER XIX

THE END OF THE WAR

Christmas—I Lose All My Belongings—The "Owl Train"
—A Wedding—Furloughed—Start for Texas—Hospitality—A
Night in the Swamp—The Flooded Country—Swimming the
Rivers—In Texas—Home Again—Surrender of Lee, Johnston,
and Kirby Smith—Copy of Leave of Absence—Recapitulation
—Valuation of Horses in 1864—Finis.

ALTHOUGH we moved in a very leisurely manner in order to give General Hood a chance to put a pontoon bridge across Tennessee River and cross his infantry, artillery, and wagon trains, the enemy never came in sight of us again.

Our Christmas was spent on this march. The weather was quite cold and many of our poor soldiers had to march over frozen ground barefooted. Between the 25th day of December, 1864, and the 1st day of January, 1865, everything had crossed to the south side of the river, during a little more than a month having seen much hard service, severe fighting, and demoralizing disaster. We continued to move leisurely southward. The main army moved to Tupelo, Miss., while our command moved to Egypt Station on the Mobile & Ohio Railroad. After crossing the river General Ross detailed Captain H. W. Wade, of the Sixth Texas, Lieutenant Thompson Morris, of the Legion, and myself as a permanent brigade court-martial.

Egypt Station is situated in one of the richest of the black land districts. Corn was abundant, and

we remained there several days, during which time
it rained almost incessantly, but the court-martial
procured quarters in a house and was able to keep
out of the black mud, which was very trying on the
men in camp. Being scarce of transportation for
baggage when we started to Georgia, the officers'
trunks and valises, containing all their best clothes,
were left in Mississippi in charge of a detail of two
men, afterwards reduced to one. While we were moving out of Tennessee the baggage was run up to a
small station on the Mobile & Ohio Railroad, and just
before we reached it a small scouting party of the
enemy's cavalry swooped down, fired the station, and
all our good clothes went up in smoke. In fact,
this and Kilpatrick's raid left me with almost " nothing to wear."

Leaving Egypt, we moved slowly back to our old
stamping-ground in the Yazoo country. We camped
one night some seventy-five miles north of Kosciusko,
and in the morning, before the command was ready
to move, about 180 men from the brigade, including
several from Company C, Third Texas, mounted
their horses and moved out, without leave, and started
for the west side of the Mississippi River. They had
organized what they were pleased to call an " owl
train," a term of no significance worth explaining.
It meant that they had become demoralized and impatient for the promised furlough, and had determined to go home without leave. It was a source of
great regret to see numbers of men who had been
good soldiers for fully three and a half years thus
defiantly quit the command with which they had so
faithfully served, but not a harsh word was said to

them, nor was effort made to stop them. Whether they would have returned or not, I do not know; perhaps many of them would, but circumstances were such that they never did. To this day many of them, perhaps all, live in constant regret that they were induced to take this one false step when we were so near the end.

On the same morning Lieutenant William H. Carr and myself obtained permission to go ahead of the command, to have some boots made, and started for Mr. Richburg's shop. A little after night the second day we reached the house of Mr. Savage, and obtained permission to spend the night. Soon after we were seated by a splendid blazing fire, his daughter, Miss Hattie, whom I had met at Mr. Blunt's about eighteen months before, came into the room. She recognized me very readily, and was apparently glad to meet me again. As there was to be a wedding at their house in about three days, she very cordially invited us to attend, which we agreed to do, provided we remained in the neighborhood that long. We hurried on to Richburg's shop, ordered our boots, which he promised to make right away—that is, in about three days. We then went to the home of my friends, the Ayres family, and made that our home for the time being. The wedding was attended by us, in company with Miss Andrews, the step-daughter, and our boots were finished just in time to enable us to join the wedding party at the dinner given the next day in Kosciusko, ten miles on our way. Here we dined, after which, bidding farewell to our friends and acquaintances, we hastened on to overtake our command.

Unexpectedly, a little later, we were favored with an order to furlough one-half of the command, officers and men, it being my fortune to be of the " one-half." Selecting and sending up the names of those to be furloughed, writing up and returning the papers, consumed time, so that it was February before we were ready to start to Texas. Lieutenant-Colonel Jiles S. Boggess, of the Third Texas, being the ranking field officer to go, was to be nominally in charge of the furloughed men, and as he lived in Henderson, my expectation was to go home with him; but it turned out otherwise. The day for starting was agreed on, leaving Colonel Boggess to bring my papers and meet me at Murdock's ferry on Yazoo River. I left camp the day before and went up to the home of John F. Williams and spent the night. John F. Williams had been sheriff of Cherokee County, Texas, in an early day, but had moved back to Mississippi. His two sons had joined our company, but Wyatt, the older one, being physically disqualified, had been discharged. He was anxious to come to his grandfather in Marshall, Texas, and I loaned him a horse on which to make the trip; and, declining to bring my boy Jake on so long a ride, to return so soon (as I then believed), I gave him a horse and saddle and told him to take care of himself.

Starting next morning with Wyatt Williams, I came on to Lexington and spent the night at the residence of our " Aunt Emma Hays." Mrs. Hays was one of the noblest women we met in Mississippi, a great friend to Ross's brigade collectively, and a special friend to a good many of us individually.

Her good old mother, Mrs. West, was there. She had lived in Marion, Ala., and was strongly attached to persons of my name there, and would always insist that I favored them, and was related to them; and the good, kind-hearted creature would do all she could for me and seemed to regret that she could not do more. These two kindly ladies furnished me luncheon enough to have lasted me, individually, almost to Rusk.

The next day we rode in the rain all day to Murdock's ferry, where, as we arrived after dark, it required a good deal of yelling and waiting to get a boat to cross in. Finally we stopped at Colonel Murdock's gate and, although his house appeared to be full of soldiers, we were welcome. Murdock was the big-hearted man who, when the brigade camped on his premises for a day and night, refused to sell the man sweet potatoes, but said: "Go back and tell the boys to come up to the house and get as many as they want." I had made the acquaintance of Mrs. Murdock and her sister, Miss Ford, of Louisiana, who was visiting her, at Lexington some months previous. I found Captain Sid Johnson, of Tyler, was at Mrs. Murdock's home. Mrs. Murdock whispered to me and said: "Supper will soon be ready for the company, but I wish you and Captain Johnson to wait and eat with the family." This we did, and afterwards were invited into the parlor, and pleasantly entertained by the ladies, Mrs. Murdock the while urging me to remain and spend my leave of absence with them instead of going to Texas.

In the meantime the rain continued to pour down,

and increased in violence, continuing all next day and the next night. While the others all pushed on except Williams and myself, I remained there until afternoon. About noon Colonel Boggess reined up at the gate long enough to say " Come ahead," and rode off in a torrent of rain, and the next time I saw him he was in Henderson, his home. Finally Williams and I started, intending to cross Sunflower Swamp and Sunflower River that evening, but soon found the whole country was overflowed, and losing much valuable time in trying to cross a creek without swimming it we had to lay out in the swamp that night. We cut a lot of cane for our horses to stand on, and piled a lot up by an old tree, and on that we sat down all night in the rain.

Next morning by swimming a large creek we reached Sunflower River, found it bank full, the ferryboat on the west side, and the ferryman gone. By going down the river three or four miles we found a farm and a private ferry, but it was afternoon when we crossed. Reaching the Mississippi we found a number of the men waiting to get over, but Colonel Boggess had crossed and gone on. The crossing was tedious in the extreme, as the only means of doing so was to swim the horses by the side of a skiff, and this had to be done in the daytime, when you had to look out for gunboats. When over, it was very uncertain with whom you were going. to travel, as every fellow, when he got his horse up the bank and over the levee on the west side, at once struck out for Texas. I lost Williams and never saw him afterwards.

The country between the Mississippi and Red

River was practically afloat. We crossed a great many streams, how many I do not remember, and we found but one stream, Little River, where the bridge was not washed away. We traveled along near the Arkansas and Louisiana line, sometimes in one State and sometimes in the other, The first stream encountered after crossing the Mississippi was a large bayou in the bottom, which we crossed on a raft constructed of logs tied together. We ferried Ouachita River, two miles, crossed Little River on a bridge, and had to swim every other stream, averaging something like three a day. We struck Red River at Carolina Bluff, some twenty miles above Shreveport, and had to swim the overflow in several places to get down to Shreveport, where we found dry ground. We came through it all with but one serious accident, and that was the drowning of a negro boy. I traveled mostly with Dr. Blocker, of Harrison County, and three or four of the Third Texas from Smith County.

One morning I found my horse badly foundered, so that I could not keep up with my crowd. Coming to Magnolia, Ark., about noon, I had to sell one of my pistols in order to trade for a horse that was able to bring me on.

Upon reaching Henderson, about eleven o'clock one day, the first man I recognized on the street was Lieutenant-Colonel Jiles S. Boggess, of the Third Texas Cavalry. He abused me roundly for being behind, and threatened that I should never leave the town with whole bones unless I went down to his house and took a rest and dinner with him, and I yielded. Here I learned that the " owl train " gang had not yet reached Texas, that they crossed the river, had been arrested at Alexandria, perhaps, and were detained under guard at Shreveport. Through the influence of Colonel Boggess, however, they were soon afterwards released by General Smith and allowed to come home.

I reached Rusk a little before noon the next day.

The following is a true copy of the paper on which I came to Texas:

HD. QTS. ROSS BRIG. CAV.,
Deasonville, Miss., Feb. 20, 1865.

Special orders
    No. 2.   Ext.

By authority from Lieutenant-General Taylor Leaves of absence are granted to the following named officers for Sixty (60) days.   .   .   .

XXVII Lieutenant S. B. Barron, Company " C " Third Texas.

L. S. Ross,
Brig. Gen'l.

At the proper time I presented myself to Colonel Boggess at Henderson, and reported to him that I was ready to start back. He told me he had no idea that we could cross the river, as it was reported to be from five to twenty-five miles wide; that he had sent a man to ascertain whether it was possible for us to cross it, and if so he would let me know, and directed me to return to Rusk and remain until I heard from him. Thus matters stood until the startling news reached us that General R. E. Lee had surrendered his army in Virginia. This was followed in quick succession by the surrender of General Joseph E. Johnston in North Carolina, the other commanding officer, and finally by General E. Kirby Smith's surrender of the trans-Mississippi department.

And then—then the four years' war, with all its fun and frolic, all its hardships and privations, its advances and retreats, its victories and defeats, its killing and maiming, was at an end.

I am unable to give the losses of Ross' brigade sustained in the Atlanta campaign. If it was ever given out officially I never saw it. But our ranks were very much depleted as the result of this long campaign. Some went to the hospitals badly wounded, some were furloughed with wounds not considered dangerous, some were rolled in their blankets and buried where they fell, and others were carried to Northern prisons, there to die or remain until the close of the war.

Nor can I now give the loss we sustained in the Nashville campaign. It was carefully made up in detail, but I do not remember it. I remember that John B. Long, of Company C, was shot through both thighs, and I remember two gallant members of Company B, Bud McClure and Joe Robinson, were killed near Pulaski on the retreat.

The regulation that our horses should be listed and valued now and then, to show the estimation placed upon horseflesh in the currency of our Government, I give the following valuations made in the early part of the year 1864, of the officers and men then present for duty, viz.:

Captain John Germany, one bay horse, $2000; Lieutenant W. H. Carr, one sorrel horse, $1200; Lieutenant R. L. Hood, one sorrel horse, $1600; Lieutenant S. B. Barron, one black horse, $1400; one bay mule, $1000; First Sergeant John B. Long, one bay horse, $900; Second Sergeant R. L. Barnett, one sorrel mare, $1500; First Corporal D. H. Allen, one sorrel horse, $1600; S. D. Box, one bay horse, $1500; Stock Ewin, one sorrel horse, $2500; J. J. Felps, one brown mule, $900; Luther Grimes, one sorrel horse, $1400; J. B. Hardgraves, one sorrel horse, $1500; J. R. Halbert, one sorrel mare, $1200; J. T. Halbert, one gray horse, $1500; W. H. Higginbotham, one gray horse, $1200; J. H. Jones, one bay mare, $1000; W. H. Kellum, one brown mule, $900; S. N. Keahey, one gray horse, $1100; G. A. McKee, one sorrel mule, $1400; Jno. Meyers, one dark roan horse, $800; Tom Petree, one sorrel horse, $1100; J. B. Reagan, one black mule, $900; C. M. Roark, one sorrel horse, $1200; A. B. Summers, one black horse, $1500; J. W. Smith, one brown horse, $1600; E. S. Wallace, one bay horse, $1600; J. R. Watkins, one sorrel horse, $2000; C. Watkins, one cream horse, $1200; T. F. Woodall, one sorrel horse, $1000; R. F. Woodall, one sorrel horse, $1600; J. W. Wade, one gray horse, $1800; T. H. Willson, one gray mule, $1000; E. W. Williams, one sorrel horse, $1400; N. J. Yates, one black mule, $1000.

THE END

ImTheStory.com

CPSIA information can be obtained at www.ICGtesting.com
Printed in the USA
BVOW03s0309190913

331595BV00015B/787/P

9 781313 878456